NEGOTIATE
with
FENG SHUI

Feng Shui for Negotiations?

If you thought that feng shui was just interior design, think again! You can use the ancient Chinese art of feng shui to achieve a successful resolution to any negotiation—from everyday interpersonal relationships to international peace treaty negotiations.

Negotiate with Feng Shui is unlike any other feng shui book. Author Jose Armilla shows you how to apply feng shui techniques to everyday situations like buying a car or asking for a pay raise. Using the straightforward techniques presented in this book, you will:

- Learn how to sense positive and negative chi in the body and in the environment

- Discover the secret to picking auspicious times and dates for important meetings

- Learn how to feng shui your present house as well as your dream house, including examples of positive and negative layouts

- Get tips on bargaining—everywhere from the flea market to the Internet

- Learn ancient blessings that improve the vibrations of the meeting place

This book is a must-read for any businessperson, arbitrator, or anyone else who wants to improve their negotiation skills and take the chance out of so-called "lucky breaks."

About the Author

A naturalized American, Jose Armilla had a passion for American English as a schoolboy in Cebu City, Philippines. He received a BA in psychology from the University of Oregon and a Ph.D. in social psychology from the University of Michigan.

In spirited American English, Armilla presents a fresh look at negotiation, using the ancient secrets of feng shui. His negotiation experience included preparing research proposals, meeting with potential sponsors, and as an American government official, he negotiated with foreign professionals. In South Vietnam, he frequently met with leaders of the Chinese business community in Cholon. During off-hours, he honed his bargaining skills with rug merchants, peddlers, itinerant art dealers, and rare seashell merchants. Armilla has been published in professional journals, most recently in the *Foreign Service Journal*. He lives in Vienna, Virginia, is married and has a daughter, a son, and two grandsons.

To Write to the Author

If you wish to contact the author or would like more information about this book, please write to the author in care of Llewellyn Worldwide and we will forward your request. Both the author and publisher appreciate hearing from you and learning of your enjoyment of this book and how it has helped you. Llewellyn Worldwide cannot guarantee that every letter written to the author can be answered, but all will be forwarded. Please write to:

Jose Armilla
℅ Llewellyn Worldwide
P. O. Box 64383, Dept. 1-56718-038-8
St. Paul, MN 55164-0383, U.S.A.

Please enclose a self-addressed stamped envelope for reply, or $1.00 to cover costs. If outside U.S.A., enclose international postal reply coupon.

Many of Llewellyn's authors have websites with additional information and resources. For more information, please visit our website at www.llewellyn.com.

NEGOTIATE

with

FENG SHUI

Enhance Your Skills in Diplomacy,
Business and Relationships

JOSE ARMILLA

2001
Llewellyn Publications
St. Paul, Minnesota 55164-0383, U.S.A.

First Edition
First Printing, 2001

Book design and editing by Connie Hill
Cover design by Lisa Novak
Interior art by Carrie Westfall (pp. xix, 34, 89) and Hollie Kilroy (pp. 33, 39, 43, 47, 67, 68, 73)

Library of Congress Cataloging-in-Publication Data
Armilla, Jose, 1934–
    Negotiate with feng shui: enhance your skills in diplomacy, business and relationships / Jose Armilla
        p.   cm. —
    Includes bibliographical references (p.   ) and index.
    ISBN 1–56718–038-8 (pbk)
    1. Feng Shui.   2. Negotiation—Miscellanea.   I. Title.
BF1779.F4 A76   2001
133.3'337—dc21   00-046533

Llewellyn Publications
A Division of Llewellyn Worldwide, Ltd.
P. O. Box 64383, Dept. 1-56718-038-8
St. Paul, MN 55164-0383, U.S.A.
www.llewellyn.com

Printed in the United States of America

Contents

Illustrations

Acknowledgments

This book resonates with the positive energy of helpful people at the peak of their powers.

The most influential person in feng shui is Master Lin Yun. I was introduced to him in the spring of 1980 by Dr. George Lee, now a Professor of International Business at San Francisco State University. Lin Yun shared ancient secrets with me after I handed him the traditional red envelope. Parents in Chinese and Vietnamese communities hand these red envelopes containing money to their offspring at the start of the lunar New Year to show affection and to bestow blessings. Many red envelopes later, from high-energy Tyson's Corner, Virginia, to trend-setting Berkeley, California, Master Lin Yun unlocked more ancient secrets. Dr. Lee did the Mandarin-to-English interpretation at these one-on-one meetings and gave enthusiastic support as well as valuable suggestions when I decided to begin this project.

A two-year tour of duty in Vietnam, from 1973 to 1974, gave me a firsthand look at transcendental methods derived from Chinese Taoism. For this experience, I am heavily indebted to two Saigon friends whom I had left behind, Nguyen Van Y and Ung Van Luong; fortunately, when Saigon fell to the North

Vietnamese, they escaped with their families in separate boats to Subic Bay, Philippines, and then to new homes in northern Virginia. They lost material possessions, but carried away their Asian wisdom to America.

For my historical analysis, I combed the collections of the Library of Congress and the Fairfax County, Virginia, Public Library. Whenever reference materials in London or Paris had to be consulted, globetrotting Frank Moy and Marcia Mau lent a hand. I also want to thank two scientific minds: Dr. Anupam N. Shah, a computer scientist, for the Indian perspective on the timing of negotiations; and Dr. Alain Y. Dessaint, a cultural anthropologist, for his valuable insights into cultural borrowing by Americans.

I am especially grateful to Connie Hill, my editor, for putting into practice the light touch and concise English of the American Midwest—to ensure that this book resonates with readers here and abroad.

In their own unique ways, my wife Ruth, daughter Arlene M. Campbell, and son Alex have contributed to the completion of this project.

Introduction

Be open to the paranormal—you may need it when you least expect it. I learned this lesson firsthand when I volunteered for a two-year tour of duty at the American Embassy in Saigon. After arriving on March 6, 1973, I expected to remain in Vietnam for two years, but no later than April 1975. I liked what I was doing and did not actively look for an onward assignment. My wife and two young children joined me later, in the fall of 1973.

A year later, in September 1974, I met a native of Central Vietnam with an uncanny ability for remote viewing. For a 500 *piaster* (60 cent) fee, he just looked at me without asking about specific concerns. Then he apparently sent his double to Washington, D.C., at the speed of thought. After a short pause, he reported what his double had detected—8,000 miles away—possibly at the office of Foreign Service personnel: "Already being prepared is an order for your new assignment. You will soon receive a message to this effect." He also added that I was going to a cold country other than the United States. His parting words were that I was exposing my family to a "nonspecific risk." Indeed, an offer arrived by official telegram on October 12 and, after some negotiation, I accepted it. This negotiation with the Assignments Officer in Washington had intu-itively factored in a "nonspecific risk." Unbeknownst to both of us, Hanoi's ruling Politburo had finally had enough, and decided on October 8 "to completely lib-erate the South." My family and I left Saigon in November on direct transfer to the American Embassy in Santiago for a tour of duty in Concepcion, gateway to the cold, but beautiful, lakes region of southern Chile. This move, with paranormal blessings, spared us from untimely evacuation before the Communist takeover on April 30, 1975.

Seven years after that demonstration by an untu-tored Vietnamese, I participated in another remote viewing exercise, in Falls Church, Virginia, performed by a sophisticated, yet accessible professor of Chinese philosophy. Out of the blue, a Chinese American friend invited my wife and me for potluck dinner at his house to meet a visitor named Lin Yun. Guests brought home-cooked dishes and, after dinner, had a one-on-one meeting with the visitor who was reputed to have supernatural powers. The icebreaker at this meeting was the red envelope presentation (see Fig. 2, p. xix). When my turn came, Lin Yun sensed a heavy dose of skepticism on my part. He said that I was test-ing him. He then accommodated me by sending his double at the speed of thought to my own house seven miles away. He said that in one bedroom of the house there was a carved wooden headboard that was broken, but the split was repaired so that now it was in use again with the bed. "Yes," I admitted to him, "there is a carved baroque headboard that a mover had carelessly handled and broken in half. But my wife eventually glued them together." Little did I know then that someday I would be writing a book applying Lin Yun's teachings.

A paranormal component is probably present in every negotiation. For example, personal chemistry between negotiators is generally regarded as a vital ingredient for concluding an agreement, but assessing this chemistry has been elusive. This book offers an empirically testable method of measuring compatibility between negotiators based on Chinese classical thought. The measurement between pairs is made possible with information on birth dates from 1870 to 2050 (so that this book may be a valued reference for a long time to come). To illustrate how the measurement works: When I arrived in Saigon, the American Ambassador was the distinguished veteran diplomat, Ellsworth Bunker, born on May 11, 1894. His nickname among the Vietnamese was "The Refrigerator," as his well-known Yankee reserve contrasted sharply with the stereotype of the gregarious, backslapping American. Following the procedure in this book (See Exercise No. 6, p. 94), the reader will discover that Ambassador Bunker and the younger President Thieu (born December 24, 1924) were compatible negotiators throughout Thieu's administration. Indeed, they were compatible, as evidenced by Bunker's six-year tenure in Saigon, from 1967 to 1973. By happy coincidence, the ambassador also hit it off with me (Fig. 1, page xvi).

Turning now to ordinary life situations, I recently played the part of chairperson in negotiations to divide the real estate properties of my paternal grandmother, who died without a will. I had the option of holding the meeting at a long dining room table with stiff-backed chairs, or keeping it in the living room with easy chairs and sofas. Under the circumstances, such a meeting of

(Photo: U.S. Information Service Saigon)

Figure 1. Ellsworth Bunker, U.S. ambassdor to the Republic of Vietnam, and author Jose Armilla, photographed together in Saigon, 1973. (Man in background unidentified.)

relatives would have been extremely stressful. We needed a paranormal stress buster. So we met in the living room and I made sure to position my easy chair in the "power spot for negotiation," a location to be identified later in the book. The result was that, as my relatives scrambled first for their perceived choice properties, what I really wanted for my share literally fell into my lap. This experience with win-win negotiation, among others, spurred me to complete this work.

A recurring theme in this book is that the ancient knowledge under discussion, including paranormal practices, came to China from Tibet where it was tested and refined over the centuries. Two pertinent questions arise: First, how could a non-Chinese author wrest these secrets without going directly to the heartland? Second, how should the author properly share the secrets with interested readers?

The answer to the first question is that you don't have to go to China at all. Ironically, authorities in Mainland China and Taiwan have dismissed these secrets as ancient superstitions to be treated with benign neglect. I have never visited China, but I had been in close contact with the customs and beliefs of *ancient* China through the overseas Chinese who have zealously preserved their heritage. You'll find them, as I did: in Cholon, the Chinese suburb of Saigon; in the shadow of Singapore's skyscrapers; in the Temple Street night market in Kowloon, Hong Kong; inside the Taoist temples of Cebu, Philippines; and inside the Black Hat Tantric Buddhist temple of Berkeley, California. At these far-flung locations, ancient knowledge continues to flourish without fear of censorship or ridicule.

Regarding the second question on sharing, I suggest we follow Lin Yun's way. Ancient knowledge is passed on through a one-on-one relationship between master and student in the reclusive monastic tradition. As a youngster in Beijing in the 1930s, Lin Yun received his first exposure to Tantric Buddhism from the Lama Ta-Teh at the Yong He Palace monastery. Later he studied under such revered Black Hat sect masters as Cheng Kuei-Ying. Despite having absorbed so much esoteric knowledge, a master does not put on airs with a client. He or she disdains the sanctimonious demeanor of a religious fanatic. The openness and compassion of the master are authentic. You gain entré by presenting him or her with a red envelope containing a token amount of money—the traditional lunar New Year offering to elicit filial piety and diligence (see Fig. 2, opposite).

Warning on Secrecy and the Red Envelope

The oral transmission of feng shui wisdom from master to client is the ideal. But a master never gives unsolicited free advice. The client must first present a red envelope containing money, and then ask the master for the most auspicious location for a house or a business. An economist might see this as the invisible hand of pure economic exchange being activated, but what the red envelope does is provide protection to the master against the negative energy of unscrupulous individuals (lacking filial piety and personal integrity) and at the same time shows sincerity and respect on the part of the client. This mutual reinforcement of positive energies is expected to enhance the success of the client's project. Paying money for this book is the substitute for the red envelope. Blessings and insights are

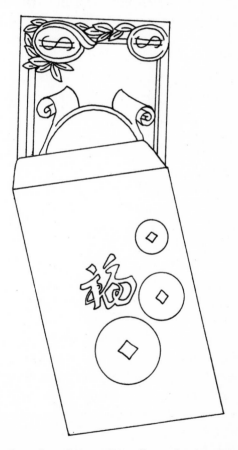

Figure 2. The red envelope traditionally used in presenting a gift of money.

bestowed on you, the reader-buyer, in return for the sincere quest for feng shui wisdom. Your purchase decision helps improve the chances of your success, but don't share the knowledge unless you have spent your own money on this book and you were asked first. Don't volunteer information on the secret methods. Violating this precept of Black Hat Tantric Buddhist feng shui could adversely diminish your own negotiating power.

Part One

■

SECRET FENG SHUI METHODS

One

■

FENG SHUI
IN ACTION

All of you have probably tried your hand at some kind of negotiation at one time or another . . . maybe without even realizing it. As a student, maybe you negotiated with a teacher to obtain a higher grade on a paper. Or as a car buyer, you might have worked judiciously with the sales person to lower the car's sticker price. Or then again, as a son, daughter, husband, or wife, perhaps you talked slowly and persuasively to obtain some wish or desire close to your heart. In fact, it would probably be hard for you to go through one day without performing some kind of informal negotiation with somebody in your life. And you don't just want to talk; you want to succeed. You may look to the worlds of negotiation, as in business or politics, to pick up tips that you can use in your more personal dealings. But even if you could talk to these experts, they probably look upon their skills as privileged information, not to be shared with the likes of you. Some of them may not even be aware of those inherent qualities that make them skilled negotiators, and couldn't tell you about them even if they wanted to. But do not despair. Help is on the way in the form of this book.

A modern authority, Thomas Colosi of the American Arbitration Association, defines negotiation as a "decision-making process in which the parties across the table decide the outcome by themselves."[1] This notion rules out any decisive influence of interested parties who are not at the negotiating table. This "here-and-now situation" shapes the negotiator's goals, strategies, intermediate objectives, and eventual tactics. Ancient Chinese secrets are in full agreement with this modern view of negotiation when the location is considered a key ingredient. Timing and the personal compatibility of both sides are also important.

Part One of this book contains those secret methods that you can use to improve your negotiations in everyday life. These secrets promote successful agreements between participants in all kinds of personal relationships in everyday affairs. Chinese officials used these very same secrets in their first negotiation with American diplomats in 1844. The Americans, arriving in a flotilla of U.S. Navy warships, had alarmed the Imperial Court. The Chinese worried about the presence of so much loose firepower in the hands of uninvited barbarians. The Chinese responded by unilaterally choosing the auspicious time and place for negotiation. They let the Americans cool their heels for four months. When they finally met with them, they arranged to have their discussions at the sacred inner shrine of a Chinese temple. The dealmaker turned out to be a windowless room with one door. There they concluded a Treaty of Friendship and Commerce that eventually guided Sino-American relations until World War II. Though the Americans were puzzled by the Chinese's diplomatic behavior, they clearly benefited from its power to move the talks expeditiously and produce an agreement of high quality. This book lifts the veil of secrecy that has existed for centuries.

In Part Two, the effectiveness of these secret methods is illustrated in vignettes from diplomatic history that demonstrate both successful and failed negotiations. These vignettes are based on factual historical records. They were packed with drama because the stakes were high. Failure in such negotiations often created great tensions, and even wars. Behind most political negotiations is the threat of force. Effectiveness in negotiation is ultimately measured not only by the mere balance of forces, but also by the close cooperation in implementing an agreement.

When diplomats sit down with their opposite numbers, they adjust to the atmospherics in the room. They react to décor—its coldness or its tastefulness. They read the other side's body language and often mirror each other's speaking rate and volume. They try to penetrate their counterpart's perspective as they seek ways to produce an agreement. Thus, empathy is a key diplomatic skill. Another is the ability to think systemically. Each side knows only too well the larger system to which they owe their loyalty—the foreign affairs establishment, its political leaders, and even the ordinary voters. Moreover, both sides are conscious of the glare of the media and the expectations of other third parties.

The ancient secrets suggest that before and during negotiation, dynamic forces could be harnessed to aid the negotiators to think in a systemic way, to avoid zero-sum conflict (one wins to the extent that the other loses), and to strive for win-win solutions. For a modern down-to-earth illustration, consider the informal negotiation that takes place on the typical school dance floor. According to dance etiquette, girls should maintain their reserve, while hopefully scouting the field. The boys should take the initiative in approaching the girls. However, the prettier the girl, the more the boy feels a strong fear of rejection. Whom to ask for a dance? The win-lose solution is to ask an unattractive wallflower; in this case, she wins and he loses (mostly his pride). But there is a shyness cure as well as a negotiation tactic. At Saturday night dances in Russian military schools, a cadet would customarily pick up a chair and dance with it as the music begins. When he spots an admiring glance from the prettiest girl, he makes his move. This indirect approach often leads to a win-win situation—the shy cadet dances with a beautiful partner.

Like a good computer program, these ancient Chinese secrets do two things. First, they automatically consider multiple factors behind win-win negotiations. Second, they give appropriate weight to all factors including location (*ti tian*), compatibility (*hsiang rong*) and timing (*chun shi*)—key ingredients to the ancient

Chinese, but often overlooked by others, in every negotiation.

American officials tend to select locations with an eye to protocol, logistics, and security. The timing of meetings is relegated to random, bureaucratic planning. The compatibility of principal negotiators remains an educated guess. However, there is one great exception to these practices in U.S. diplomatic history—the summit meeting in Geneva, November 19–21, 1985, between President Ronald Reagan and Soviet General Secretary Mikhail Gorbachev. Reagan's time of arrival, media briefing schedule, and meetings with the Soviet leader were determined in advance, transcendentally and secretly, by a San Francisco astrologer working for the Reagans. There was also an attempt to assess in advance the two leaders' personal chemistry. The meeting places were lucky. This book will show that President and Mrs. Reagan utilized an ancient wisdom that is similar to the systemic thinking of some ancient Chinese teachers.

This book is about tapping into hidden energies in your surroundings and within yourself so that you can implement them for your own happiness. You don't have to be a diplomat, a labor union negotiator, or a business mogul. Best of all—you can use these secret methods in everyday life anywhere in the world.

What Is Feng Shui?

Feng shui (pronounced "fung shoo-ay") literally means "wind and water." Master Yang Yun-Sang, who lived

around A.D. 888 during the Tang Dynasty, first popularized this term. He needed a catch phrase to describe
the work he was doing for his employer, the Tang
Emperor Hi Tsang. He advised the Emperor on im-per-
ial building projects, including gravesites, and overall
city planning. As the author of early books on feng
shui, he emphasized the need to design buildings and
houses so that their occupants will live in harmony
with the visible and invisible forces of nature. As environmental forces, wind and water have the joint potential to harm or help people in their homes. The
harmful side is, of course, exemplified by the typhoon.
Strong wind gusts usually create high waves that can
destroy homes along the shores, and heavy rains can
cause landslides and flooding.

On the other hand, the helpful side of wind and
water can be illustrated in a modern invention. In the
privacy of some upscale American bathrooms, a fifty-
fifty mixture of air and water whirling around a
designer bathtub buoys the human spirit with its relax-
ing massage action. This is the modern whirlpool tub,
popular among customers dedicated to personal hygiene. Next to cleanliness, however, one whirlpool
model promises a shiatsu massage. Shiatsu is a form
of therapeutic massage that applies pressure on the
acupuncture points so as to balance the body's chi
energy. To demonstrate this restorative power of air
and water, a familiar ritual may be briefly described. At
day's end, an American soccer mom is probably near
complete exhaustion, yet she frequently gains a second
wind after immersing herself in her whirlpool tub.[2]

The soccer mom's secret can be found in the numerous microjets that knead her back with warm water. She discovers hidden reserves of energy during this whirlpool bath. These hidden reserves are part of the unseen chi energy. Her bodily chi balances harmoniously with the enveloping chi of the air and water mixture. Clearly, chi is an attribute of animate as well as inanimate objects. As Master Yang might say if he were alive today, "You and I have chi, and so does the whirlpool tub."

Chi is an unseen energy and, like air, it has weight or mass as a quantifiable physical attribute. For the weight-conscious reader, Western researchers had determined that what we call human chi, when it goes "out-of-body," weighs approximately two-and-a-half ounces—about equal to a small pack of fat-free gelatin mix.[3] Once back in a living human body, chi may be detected as balanced or smooth, or rising or flowing downward, sometimes by looking at the eyes and complexion, and by listening to the quality of the voice. Chi has no shape, color, size, sound, smell, or taste. All things have chi; therefore, it is not a defining trait of human beings. In this book, phrases such as "chi flow," "misguided chi," or "chi adjustment" describe the interplay between people and their surroundings. There is a chi spectrum, with environmental chi at one end and human chi or spirit at the other. When a person's chi is blocked by his or her inauspicious surroundings, a sincere search for feng shui wisdom is highly recommended. *In the strict sense of the term, feng shui is the ancient Chinese art of balancing the chi energy in the environment with the flow of a person's chi in order to increase his or her effectiveness in human affairs.*

This book will promote an intuitive knowledge as well as practical application of feng shui. Very little theory will be discussed. While there are numerous schools of thought about feng shui, this book is guided by one particular school. It is the feng shui practiced by the Black Hat Sect of Tibetan Tantric Buddhism, represented in the United States by Master Lin Yun.[4] In this book, Black Hat Tantric Buddhist feng shui is the term used to distinguish it from traditional feng shui such as the Compass School. Tantras are the scriptures in Tibetan Buddhism; tantra literally means "to weave" in Sanskrit, and thus refers to the interweaving and interdependence of all things and events. Tibetan spiritual teachers went to Beijing under imperial patronage during the Ming (A.D. 1368–1644) and the Ching (A.D. 1644–1911) dynasties, and their teachings were based on meditation and secret cures. They were embedded in traditional feng shui in order to appeal to their imperial patrons.

Since then feng shui has gone in new directions. Traditional feng shui emphasizes only shapes and directions at negotiations. For example, very long rectangular tables are unlucky for negotiation; a principal negotiator should have his or her back against a solid straight wall, not against a door or window; and the negotiator should face the compass direction predetermined by his or her astrological sign. In contrast, Black Hat Tantric Buddhist feng shui dispenses with the compass—it does not depend on it to locate a lucky direction. Instead, its feng shui masters prefer to orient themselves from the main door of a boardroom to find a negotiator's power spot. More importantly, these feng shui masters believe that transcendental intervention could change the unlucky aspects of certain shapes and directions. This transcendental factor is chi adjustment. Chi adjustment might include a ritual performed by a master whose ability to manipulate chi energy in a positive manner blesses the meeting room. In the hands of a master, this chi adjustment within the boardroom can improve the give-and-take discussion among participants, culminating in a successful negotiation.

In some instances of chi adjustment, the feng shui master need not make a house call. For example, antique Tibetan Buddhist statues and paintings have found their way into some well-to-do and well-sited American homes, and have energized their occupants in a transcendental way—they have prospered even more. Tibetan lamas had meditated and chanted before these protective images, thereby releasing their chi directly onto each sculpture or painting. The luminous chi of the lamas had been stored in these objects over the centuries. These high-energy religious treasures directly affected the homeowners' chi and helped bring to fruition their talent for making money.[5] However, if you ask these Americans to account for their prosperity, they would tell you more about hard work and business savvy than about a chi adjustment blessing the home.

The Foyer's Chi Energy

The entrance is the best place to feel the chi energy circulating throughout a house. Almost all feng shui masters would agree that a spacious and well-lighted foyer, with minimal dècor, could probably induce positive vibes on the first-time visitor. If you were this visitor, your shoulders would be relaxed; your breathing would be normal, not heavy, without a wheezing sound; the pupils of your eyes would be somewhat dilated. You would make immediate eye contact with the welcoming homeowner. You are clearly upbeat. This is known as "the bright-hall effect." Suppose you have just entered a large modern house through a well-proportioned door that opens to a two-story foyer. In this case, the foyer is considered the tai chi area, the center of the chi energy swirling around the house interior. Stepping into the eye of the storm, you feel a quiet, understated elegance within a high-energy environment. The vibrations are distinctly positive. In contrast, a dimly lit and confining foyer would probably lead to a glazed look in your eyes, breathing difficulties, and a slight headache as the unlucky ambiance sends your own chi energy downhill.

Two

■

GO WITH THE CHI FLOW

A feng shui master seeks to infuse his or her client with positive energy by redirecting chi from the immediate surroundings where he or she spends the most time. An ordered list of this chi-rich environment usually begins with:

Bed
Bedroom
House
Yard
Neighborhood
District
City/State/Province
Country
Earth
The Universe

If you are a workaholic, your office desk and workplace lead the list, followed by your bed and bedroom at home. If you are a road warrior-negotiator, hotel beds and suites rank highly. Indeed, as you prepare for prolonged negotiations, you should check out your hotel suite and test the bed in which you'll be sleeping as carefully as you craft a negotiation strategy. Eight to ten hours of daily sleep are required to boost your chi.

Chi Flow

In America today, the concept of chi has entered mainstream thought. Many Americans are exposed to the martial arts; to the healing arts of acupuncture, chi gong and yoga—and to inspirational books on the ancient wisdom of China, Tibet, Japan, and India. "Flow your chi" and "concentrate the chi" are commonly heard exhortations of martial arts teachers, used to guide beginners and black belts alike. How to develop the chi is primarily taught from teacher to student in the oral tradition. The following exercise provides a good start on learning about chi.

Exercise No. 1
Confirmation of Chi Balance

Our chi should be smooth and balanced as long as we maintain optimum health and live in serene surroundings, but the chi can become unbalanced from time to time, much to our discomfort. Only then do we pay attention to the chi as we seek ways to overcome the discomfort. The exercises below help illuminate first the unbalanced chi and then some objective confirmation that the chi is back to normal balance.

Suppose you are in superb physical condition and manage to sleep eight to ten hours daily. You wake up one Monday morning with dry mouth, hands sweaty, and heart racing. The stressor might be an important business negotiation to begin on Wednesday or the speech you have to give on Friday. Choose an appropriate exercise below.

Negotiator's Warm-Up

You need a warm-up to control the tendency to be extremely loud and verbally aggressive during negotiations. You would wish to project the image of a critic who is thoughtful without being intolerant. The feng shui warm-up: *Every morning, take a deep breath, then exhale beginning with eight small puffs, followed by a long ninth breath. Repeat nine times daily for twenty-seven days.*

Confirmation: Well-modulated, clear tone of voice.

Tapping the Eye (infraorbital ridge)

Even seasoned speakers admit to having butterflies in the stomach when in front of an audience. By using this tapping method, these speakers would soon recover because they feel that the butterflies are now "flying in formation," energizing instead of unsettling them. You may try this when feeling extremely nervous about a speaking engagement: *Think about your upcoming speech. Using three middle fingers, gently tap the bony ridge directly below one eye, with both eyes looking straight ahead. Repeat nine times.*

Confirmation: Nervous stomach is calmed.

Pressing the "Great Eliminator"

You address yourself to an important acupuncture "point" in your body, using a shiatsu massage technique. This "point" has been called since ancient times the Great Eliminator. It helps you eliminate the discomfort indicated by your sweaty palms as you anticipate a contentious business meeting. *For ten seconds, press the point in the middle of the web of flesh between thumb and forefinger of your dominant hand, using the fingers of your nondominant hand to apply pressure.*

Confirmation: Normal heart rate returns.

Drink Up

Martial arts teachers say that after a vigorous workout you have to rebalance the chi by replacing the quart or so of water lost through perspiration. They suggest *drinking daily ten to fourteen glasses of water, sixteen glasses if possible, year-round.* "Water balance"—you take in as much water as you lose—is also a manifestation of chi balance. You can see this in the pale straw color of your urine. If it's a deeper yellow, you need to rebalance the chi with more fluids.

Confirmation: Dry mouth is gone, urine has pale straw color.

Concentrating the Chi

Martial arts training reveals the secret location of the "seat of the chi," or the "center of balance." A typical martial arts student must learn to first channel chi to flow with precision and smoothness, so that throwing a larger opponent will be effortless. If you listen in during martial arts class, this is what you will probably overhear as a teacher begins to instruct two advanced students (the "victim" and the "attacker") on how best to execute a classic form:

"When you sense an attack, you must relax and *concentrate your chi* at the point two inches below the navel and deep within the pelvis. Then, as the attacker moves in to grab your wrist and break your balance, you extend the wrist forward as bait. Now you control the timing of the contact and gain room for maneuver. You harmonize with the flow of the attacker's chi first by bending the grasped wrist and then by slightly turning your upper body. The attacker's chi now moves on a parallel course with your own. You focus your chi on the fingertips of the seized wrist that point in the same direction as the attacker's hand. The elbow is bent and relaxed, harmonizing with gravity. Your eyes and chi are then focused on the spot where you intend the attacker to land. With a sharp twist of your upper body, you abruptly throw your opponent onto the mat—for a crisp and explosive finish."

After watching the above demonstration, you might ask, "What caused the attacker's body to suddenly pop up, float in space, and fall down?" According to martial arts teachers, it is the unseen chi circulating under the student-victim's control.[1]

While communication from the teacher is primarily nonverbal, the student receives clear, positive feedback when an opponent's body hits the floor. During group exercises, each student resonates with the chi of the teacher and with the chi of advanced students in choreographed, swirling movements. This rhythmic flow of teacher's chi and black belt's chi helps develop a beginner's skills through chi adjustment.

Chi Adjustment

Chi adjustment is best illustrated in *chi gong*, which is a blend of meditation and movement exercises to achieve bodily health and harmony. Chi gong practice releases chi, which has mass, and thus could accumulate over time in an external object such as the chi gong master's jacket. In one instance, a master asked his American students to take turns in putting on his chi-rich jacket. Most of them reported high-energy stimulation from wearing it even for a few seconds.[2] Thus, chi adjustment is a high-energy stimulation received from auspicious surroundings and/or individuals.

Beaches and lush, green parks are ideal outdoor classrooms for martial arts because they activate the smooth circulation of environmental energy with which both the teacher and the student can harmonize. It was such an auspicious place of positive energy—the environs of the Shao Lin temple in Henan Province, China—which gave rise to the kung fu innovations that have spread around the world.

Seat of the Chi

In Chinese classical teaching, the seat of the chi is located in the lower abdomen, about two inches below the navel—called *tan den* in Chinese, *hara* in Japanese.

It is the person's center of gravity, equilibrium, and power. Like a martial arts enthusiast, the negotiator should be focused first on the hara, the belly. From this strong and balanced center, the chi flows freely out through the arms and hands, and upward to the head, preparing him or her for deal making. In fact, power brokers in Japan—key bureaucrats and politicians—are renowned practitioners of *haragei*, the "art of the belly." It is the art of empathizing with others and satisfying their concerns while pursuing one's own interests.

Haragei is mainly nonverbal communication. The speaker says just a few words that carry a complex message, but growing up in the same culture, the listener gets information from understanding what the speaker should be saying in contrast to what he is actually saying. For example, a top bureaucrat might meet with farmers' groups to reassure them that the government would continue its generous subsidy to rice farmers. But the underemployed farmer who gets paid for producing nothing understands what the speaker should be saying—that farmers like him or her should move to the city and get a factory job. The bureaucrat-negotiator's haragei has been very effective: in 1950, some 60 percent of the Japanese lived on farms, but today farmers make up no more than 2–3 percent of the work force, as in the United States. Many apparently voted with their feet to give up farming, with some indirect persuasion through haragei.

Three

■

TIMING

Feng shui as the unseen player in negotiation is not a form of psychological warfare to increase situational stress to the disadvantage of the other side. Rather it is intended to help both sides boost their empathy, sensitivity, and responsiveness to the other's concerns. The emphasis on auspicious room layout, compatibility, and perfect timing is beneficial to both parties. The feng shui perspective means that you have to look at negotiations in a different light. Take, for instance, the element of timing, a lesson informally taught in many cultures.

First Footing

In the Scottish Highlands, a special visitor is welcomed on New Year's Day for bringing good luck to the house. A kind of "homeowner's insurance policy," he arrives in the person of a distinguished male dressed in kilts, carrying a lump of coal. This is the Scottish custom of "first footing on the threshold." The Scots believe that the first male visitor on New Year's Day has the power

to bestow good fortune on the family for the remain-
der of the year. Some male visitors carry a higher pre-
mium than others, based on Highland historical
experience. In the South, a blond is preferred over a
dark-haired male, a holdover of the region's frequent
brushes with dark-haired English invaders. In the
North, however, the dark-haired visitor is a more welcome sight, for he would portend prosperity rather
than plunder by the much-feared blond Nordic
invaders. Thus, "first footing" is an example of a culture teaching its members a lesson in timing to attract
good luck.

At Tet in 1974, the Year of the Tiger, I did the first
footing on the threshold of the Saigon house of a Vietnamese friend. Tet begins on New Year's Day in the
Chinese lunar calendar, the second new moon after the
winter solstice. Like the Scots on the other side of the
world, the Vietnamese believe that a distinguished person should be the first visitor to bring good luck to the
home. But unlike the Scots, the Vietnamese welcome
either male or female, provided the first visitor has a
Chinese animal sign harmonious to the homeowner's
sign, or a lucky name such as Loc (abundance) or Kim
(gold). I was invited in advance to be the guest of
honor with my wife at the Saigon family's Tet celebration. Promptly, in the morning of January 23, 1974, I
was the first person to step on the threshold of the residence carrying, not a lump of coal, but appropriate Tet
gifts including a bottle of White Horse Scotch whisky.

I was my friend's "insurance policy" for one year.
However, before the year ended, we bid each other

farewell on November 27, 1974, as I left Saigon for a new overseas assignment. He and his family were safe and comfortable in their house well after my departure, but the "insurance protection" lapsed when the Year of the Cat arrived at Tet on February 11, 1975. By April 30, 1975, my friend's extended family had fled from their residence as the Communist invaders approached Saigon. They joined the boat people on the way to freedom. After the dust settled, a Communist Viet Cong colonel and his family then took over their residence.

Timing Your Actions

In everyday negotiations, say, with a spouse, a sense of timing is required. You have to be aware of your spouse's mood swings. You might even consider the phases of the moon because from past experience you probably know he or she will not be open to reason during the full moon. In business negotiation, you should avoid travel within twenty-four hours before and after a moon or sun eclipse, or more so if the meeting itself is scheduled within that time frame. These recurring events raise a red flag among astrologers who believe that eclipses indicate a bad period for travel. When a business agreement on something is finally reached, the time of the signing ceremony is crucial. Like a marriage ceremony, an auspicious start influences the implementation and harmonious relationship between the parties. Also, like a marriage ceremony in Asian cultures, you will need an expert to suggest the most auspicious date and time in advance. If expert guidance is beyond your reach, you can consult various astrological almanacs about timing your actions: American, European, Chinese, Vietnamese, and East Indian. However, you do not have to be a believer in astrology at all. You need to consult an almanac because your opposite numbers in a negotiation might be following the guidance offered by it. For example, if your counterparts are overseas Chinese, your best bet is to check out a Chinese almanac that can be translated by native speakers as needed. At first, your counterparts might appear inscrutable. In public, they will probably say that they themselves don't believe in such superstitions as feng shui and astrology, but privately, they might have prepared for your meeting by using the tips on timing and other secrets disclosed in this book.

Rest assured, however, that the precautions given in this book are for your enjoyment. They are easy to follow, and you don't have to be a Nervous Nelly or Clockwork Charlie to do well. Before a negotiation, you may consult this book to check out the location and compatibility factors. Then seek a reliable source for timing purposes. The rest are the usual nuts-and-bolts of meticulous preparation on your part.

If you want to know more about how to develop a sense of timing, you need look no further than a golf analogy. You join a club and practice your swing daily under a pro's guidance; inside the pro shop, you read this negotiation book, and it also helps if you were born into a negotiator's family. In India, there is such a "negotiators' culture," a kind of members-only club.

You are born into what for centuries has been called the *Gujarati* culture. Children from this culture of entrepreneurs grow up with almost daily exposure to Indian astrology. Later they marry, following the custom of premarital matching of a couple's horoscopes. When they negotiate as adult business people, they probably bring to the table a win-win attitude because they have consulted the same almanac for proper timing.[1]

A Charismatic Day

A printed invitation to an annual charitable fund-raising event arrived in my mail early in April 1999. Dubbed the "Kentucky Derby Party," it was intended to lure the so-called "high rollers," as well as compassionate contributors, to participate in such activities as "picking the ponies" during the afternoon televised race at Churchill Downs on May 1,1999. It was to be held at a luxurious private residence in McLean, Virginia; it turned out to be situated midlevel on a small wooded hill, very spacious and feng-shui correct. Accepting the invitation well before the deadline, I consulted an American almanac and found that the day of the race was for me "very favorable," and for my wife "slightly favorable."[2] The "ponies" were unknown quantities to me, but on the day of the race, competing horses were shown on TV early in the afternoon, with commentaries on the betting odds. While waiting for my wife to get dressed, I turned on the TV and spotted a horse named Charismatic posed with his jockey, who was clad in a green jacket with light yellow stripes. I liked green especially, since it is the color of growth and renewal in feng shui. Charismatic's 31 to 1 odds clinched the choice for me, but I did not tell my wife about it. I wanted to observe how our own husband-wife negotiation would prosper at the betting table. On arrival at the party, we found the "off track" betting table at the sunroom adjoining the large recreation room that displayed a giant TV screen. According to the *bagua*, both rooms occupied the marriage and relationships sector of the house. When the time came for my wife to place her bets, she consulted with me. I told her to pick a horse on her own. After she did this, she decided to bet also on my horse. Charismatic won the race despite being an "unknown hay burner" ridden, according to the media, by an overweight jockey recovering from substance abuse problems. Half of the money we won went to the charitable fund. Rightly or wrongly, we attribute our win to several factors including:

- Consulting the almanac for right timing

- The green color of the jockey's jacket—symbol of growth and renewal

- Charismatic's long-shot status—siding with the underdog

- The house's good feng shui

- Compassion for the needy

Best Dates for Hassle-Free Flying

You may skip this section if you have a fear of flying and don't intend to travel by plane. The tips below don't promise to overcome any fear, even including the anxiety some frequent flyers experience now and then. The purpose of this section is to help you achieve a hassle-free flight. Even if you like to risk flight delays, missed connections, or being bumped from overbooked flights for a chance to earn free tickets, you had better avoid the worst dates and go for the best dates:

Don't begin travel within twenty-four hours of an eclipse, whether solar or lunar. Example of a traveler who flew on such a date: An elderly matriarch died during the solar eclipse on February 16, 1999. One relative then flew across the continental United States within eight hours of the death to attend the funeral, but her connecting flight was delayed and she had to stay overnight at an airport hotel before completing her journey. In contrast, several other relatives who traveled on February 17 did not experience any significant flight delays.

Consult an almanac for an auspicious date to fly. Don't give the travel agent tentative dates, or worse, leave your return flight open. Pick the best dates both for your departure and return. If you are a business traveler, your boss or client at the other end may want to tinker with your itinerary. You can use this standard negotiating tactic with the boss instead: "I checked again with the travel agent who said . . ." You fill in the best dates in the almanac, on which you have already made reservations. You'll be surprised how quickly the boss would defer to the travel specialist's "decision."

For a family traveling together, the head of the family should use his or her auspicious date.

Look for confirmation of the almanac's accuracy through-out the trip. You just relax and observe how the "self-fulfilling prophecy" of the almanac would unfold. A personal example: On a December holiday visit to California, my wife, son, and I flew from Washington's Reagan National Airport via Memphis. Our plane had been delayed because of bad weather in Boston where it originated. As a result, we missed the scheduled connecting flight to Los Angeles from Memphis. We had to wait for a late evening flight. At that point, it seemed the opposite of what the almanac said was a good day for us to fly. We had never before been to this city, which is a prolific contributor to Americana. Soon we were upbeat, despite a touch of the "Memphis blues." We toured Graceland, Elvis Presley's home, and then for supper we had our first taste of the famous Memphis pork ribs barbecue at the airline's expense. When we boarded our flight, the airline surprised us with an upgrade to first class. The in-flight dinner's piéce de résistance was delicious seafood, served on real china with fresh white linens, and accompanied by a bottle of white wine. The day ended to everyone's satisfaction. Signs confirming that you have picked a good day to fly may also include:

■ Your name is called first from the standby list (senior travelers in the U.S. on discounted tickets are wait-listed)

- You discover that you just earned a mileage bonus on your frequent flyer program for taking a connecting flight from a particular city

- A smiling ticket agent makes eye contact

- Ticket agent finds you an aisle seat in coach class with two adjacent seats unoccupied (helpful in long flights to Japan)

- Flight attendants turn on the charm while serving you

- On arriving at a Japanese airport, you find the lone Western-style toilet vacant—next to clean, but Japanese-style toilets

- At journey's end, a white-gloved taxi driver hands your luggage back with a courteous bow

Four

■

NEGOTIATING A HOUSE PURCHASE

Feng Shui Basics

To understand modern-day feng shui, you can visualize a TV screen. Shown on that screen are secret feng shui tips to help you reach successful agreements in all of your dealings. Though the color TV set in your home runs on electronic circuitry, the TV screen which you visualize in your mind operates on chi circuitry. Chi circulation is basically the flow of information and intelligence. This circuitry obeys these laws:

Wish is action

Some marathon swimmers rely on this principle to conquer fatigue. For example, a tired swimmer visualizes a relaxed double floating in the air overhead as he or she continues to swim. When the floating body rejoins the physical body, he or she feels refreshed. The wish to go beyond the usual limits of physical endurance results in swimming another mile without feeling fatigue.

31

Part is whole

A person's chi resonates with the environment. When a feng shui master detects a blocked chi in his client, he might recommend as the first-line remedy a rearrangement of the bedroom furniture. This chi adjustment illustrates the principle that a person's well-being is part of a larger unified whole.

Contact is unification

Chanting is part and parcel of Black Hat Tantric Buddhism. A ritualistic chant—mantra—allows your own small voice to make physical and spiritual contact with the larger environment. For example, in a house blessing ceremony, your voice resonates with those of other well-wishers. This group chanting invites positive natural forces in the environment to enter the house and bestow happiness and good fortune on its occupants.

Imitation is reality

When a feng shui master says that a house is sited along a path to receive *sheng* chi, the dragon's breath, he or she is invoking the "imitation-is-reality" rule. What they mean is that the house is drawing in bursts of positive chi from its auspicious surroundings. Feng shui tips are generally crisp and clear. Some advice may appear comical or "tongue-in-chi," but reject them only at your peril.

Exercise No. 2

Home Check-Up

Look at the TV screen in your mind for a moment and visualize an octagon for network identification, so to speak. This is the bagua, the mystical logo of feng shui (Fig. 3, below). Next, the logo is enlarged. You visualize a house's floor plan as though shooting with a wide-angle TV camera mounted from the ceiling, and the logo is floating overhead, filling the screen (Fig. 4, page 34). The bagua is centered on the tai chi symbol (No. 3), which denotes balanced chi (harmony and health). The bagua is always oriented to the door or *ch'i kou* ("mouth of the chi"), following the practice of the Black Hat Tantric Buddhist sect. The main door has three possible locations: career (No. 8), knowledge (No. 6), or helpful people and friends (No. 4). The other five sides of the octagon are: family (No. 1),

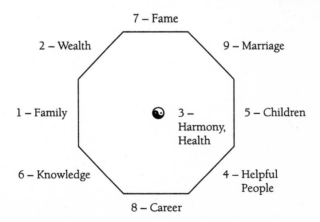

Figure 3. The bagua, the mystical logo of feng shui.

wealth (No. 2), fame (No. 7), marriage (No. 9), and children (No. 5). The numbers correspond to nine sectors that are the way stations for chi circulation within the house. Thus, your toast at a family reunion dinner: family (1), prosperity (2), good health (3), and friendships (4), intuitively reflects the bagua ranking in order of importance.

This house plan indicates that all corners are lucky. It is based on the "post-and-lintel" design of a typical Asian house. You erect four posts and connect them with beams. In contrast, the modern American house is built on the "balloon" design. You lay down a foundation, not necessarily rectangular, and construct around this foundation interlocking shells with a roof above. You may find a corner missing (inverted), say, the knowledge sector, which immediately calls for a remedy.

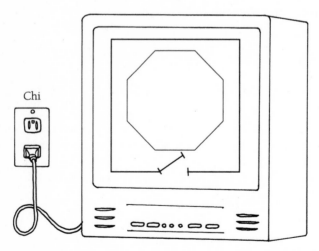

Figure 4. TV screen with the bagua logo superimposed on a house plan.

Feng Shui Your House

A typical house in an upper-middle-class American neighborhood has four bedrooms with two-and-a-half bathrooms. Your dream house should be a "move-up" house. In feng shui, you progress in many subtle ways by moving from a smaller to a bigger house, not the other way around. On the first floor of our hypothetical house are found a guest bathroom, family room, living room, dining room, and kitchen, as well as an attached two-car garage. The home checkup ideally begins with the first floor. Next, you visualize the bagua floating above the master bedroom upstairs, using the door for orientation. In this hypothetical home, you'll discover that the location of the bed is already in the marriage sector. It appears that the architect intuitively drew up the house plans by combining structural and marital stability as design elements. In short, as far as relationships are concerned, our hypothetical house has good feng shui.

Consider a young professional couple making plans to buy a house. For them, buying a house is a series of negotiations with a dynamic agenda. Their original goal may be to give themselves the best possible home that their money can buy. Then they may change their vision of house ownership and want a home that would be an investment vehicle. They may want to buy and sell, moving in and out of houses constantly in order to turn a profit. Either way, this couple can only get what it wants through negotiations with a phalanx of specialists: a builder, an architect, a contractor, a real estate agent, a lawyer, and a mortgage banker.

However, from the Black Hat Tantric Buddhist feng shui point of view, the most decisive negotiation takes place when the dream house is just a gleam in the couple's eyes. The wife wants a two-story colonial, while the husband prefers a contemporary ranch-style rambler. Secret feng shui methods could resolve such differences.

Present House

The couple's decision-making may be triggered by pillow talk in the bedroom of their present house or apartment. This pillow talk would be most auspicious if the bed is moved to the marriage sector of the bedroom. If the bed is already there, well and good. The mystical vibrations in this sector seamlessly blend the female and male qualities of human nature. In the Tantras, a wife's intuitive wisdom, a passive female quality, unites with her husband's love and compassion, an active male quality. The bagua is useful in the proper placement of the bed. It would signify happy marital relations. The bed is the closest contact that the human body has with the environment (see chapter two). The best chi is channeled directly to the couple through their bed. Positioning the bed in the marriage sector thus improves the silent dialogue between man and nature, and blesses the whispered pillow conversation between man and wife.

The house-buying tête-à-tête spills over from the bedroom to the kitchen where they spend the morning looking at house plans and prices. There the breakfast table takes on a new meaning. It is now the command center for deployment of the family wealth. In Chinese, the word for food—*chai*—sounds the same as the word for making money (in Cantonese, *faet choih* means "making money").

The placement of the stove is also crucial. Where the food is cooked is the spot for wealth accumulation. While seated at the breakfast table, the wife should have her back to the stove, so she would be willing to part with some of the family wealth in a new venture. If she faces the stove, she would remain the conservative cook—increasing, protecting, and never taking risks with the family's assets. The husband should sit catty-corner to the door in the kitchen. However, the modern kitchen is fraught with feng shui booby traps; for example, a rustic decorative touch can turn menacing—exposed structural beams with pots and pans hanging from them, which are intended to achieve the gourmet look. If the breakfast table is located below a beam, the seated couple could experience headaches, poor judgment, and costly compromises in choosing a house. In this case, the couple should move over to the formal dining room table.

Sitting away from the influence of the overhead beams in the kitchen, the husband and wife will feel their stress lifted. They will see clearly the long-term consequences of any purchase decision.

Dream House

They have narrowed their selection to two affordable houses on the market, but the houses have significantly contrasting prices. At this point, feng shui would uncover the couple's values by forcing them to make a choice on the basis of the location of the master bedroom. Both homes are sited auspiciously. The house with a lower price tag has the master bedroom located in the wealth sector. If the couple's top concern is wealth before age forty at the expense of marital bliss, then they should choose this house. They'll have money left over to buy furnishings for this dream home and avoid becoming "house poor" (see Fig. 5, page 39).

However, if a happy marriage is the highest goal, they should opt for the more expensive house with the master bedroom in the marriage sector. Another positive feature is that the toilet and the whirlpool tub in the bath adjoining the master bedroom are located away from the marriage sector itself. This placement ensures that romance will not be flushed down the drain. These fixtures generate strong water chi flowing downward—an inauspicious direction for a marriage. On the other hand, toilets and whirlpool tubs are an aid to purification and restoration of chi equilibrium. This balanced chi is noticeable when emerging from a bath; the person shows pure unblemished skin with a rosy tinge, and speaks in a soft voice and a clear tone.

Guided by such feng shui wisdom, the couple eventually agrees to buy the more expensive house that promises happy marital relations. The next negotiation

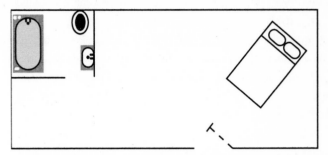

A. Downwardly mobile, but devoted couple.

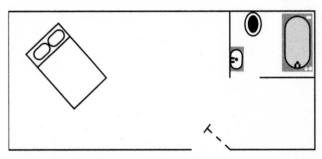

B. Upwardly mobile, but unlucky in love.

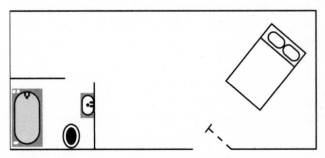

C. Happily married, well-off couple.

Figure 5. Master bedroom secrets.

involves the couple's seeking a thirty-year mortgage loan from their bank. They face the loan officer with their sides rather than their backs to the office door. It is a win-win negotiation. The couple qualifies for a relatively low interest loan with a small down payment while the mortgage banker adds to his real estate portfolio an expensive dwelling owned by a two-income couple with good jobs.

Later when the couple finally approaches the seller of the desired house through a real estate broker, the negotiation also becomes a win-win situation. The couple sits in the seller's living room catty-corner to the door. They start low—at thirty percent less than the asking price. Then the seller reduces the asking price by 15 percent—meeting them halfway for a quick sale. Thus, the buyers acquire a comfortable and feng shui-correct home.

An Effective Negotiator's House

There is a good fit between an effective negotiator and the house where he or she lives. From the feng shui perspective, a win-win negotiator is a person who wants to make enough money, to keep tension to a minimum, and to close a deal that satisfies both sides as much as possible. He or she sticks to the win-win approach because his or her *house* makes him or her comfortable with this approach.

An example is the house of a Chinese comprador, Mr. Chung, in nineteenth-century Hong Kong.[1] He worked for a British firm, the Peninsular and Oriental Steam Navigation Company. A comprador was the foreign proxy—purchasing agent, go-between, and interpreter—between his superiors and the Chinese merchants and local officials on the mainland treaty ports. It was his job to keep a good eye on profit margins and smooth bilateral trade relations. In short, he specialized in win-win negotiations. His effectiveness was judged by the way he made money for his British employer; for the Chinese suppliers and buyers, and, of course, for his own account. He lived in a feng shui-correct townhouse (Fig. 6, page 43). Shown is the main floor where he entertained friends and business associates. As his stock-in-trade was market knowledge and persuasive power, the main door was auspiciously located in the "knowledge" sector. This door was not aligned directly against the interior doors leading to the terrace which was fronting the Hong Kong harbor, thereby ensuring that the positive energy entering the house through the main door was allowed to circulate inside. If the three doors were aligned in a row, his guests would have turned argumentative, and an invisible draft would literally blow opportunities and money out to sea. Moreover, the sectors for "family" and "children" were enlarged by the townhouse design, increasing his luck in those areas. The "helpful people" sector, appropriately enough, had the cubicle for opium smoking. Opium was legal in Hong Kong until World War II, and this private "opium den" was fully stocked and available to any guest with an opium habit. In modern days, this area would be used for the wet bar and cigar smoking, a place where deals with important clients would be concluded.

The first floor public rooms of the wealthy comprador's house boast an entry staircase (A), in the
knowledge corner. In the "opium den" (B) to the right
of the entrance are chairs and a bed for guests. The
ante-chamber (C) leads to the *salle à manger* or dining
area (D), where meals are served at a large table (E),
shown with stools around it for seating. Entertainment
would be provided for guests by musicians seated to
the left of the dining area (F). At the end of the house
is an open-air terrace (G), overlooking the sea. A table
(H) is set up there with brandy, soda, pale ale, and
cigars. On the edge of the terrace are a row of potted
flowers (I), and the Hong Kong harbor (K) is just
beyond the terrace.

House Layout with Good Vibes

- *Entrance.* Curving walkway to the door, no tree
  directly aligned to the front door, back door not
  directly aligned to the front door; brightly
  lighted

- *Foyer and stairs.* Generally, the foyer next to
  the stairs is the tai chi of the house; a curving
  stairway with a two-story open foyer is ideal for
  health and harmony; when stairs are aligned to
  the entrance, chi rushes back down and out of
  the door

- *Missing corner.* If there is a missing corner in the
  house layout, such as the "wealth sector," plant
  evergreen bushes in the yard to complete the
  corner; if not corrected, this missing "wealth"
  corner would be indicative of occupants prone
  to high living from paycheck to paycheck

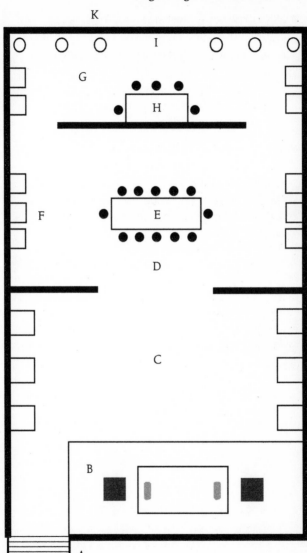

Figure 6. An effective negotiator's house.

- *Stove.* The cook must have security and command of the kitchen when facing the stove; a cook center on an island cabinet is the ideal; if the cook faces a wall, a convex mirror (available in auto parts store) should be attached to it to reflect the space in the room behind the cook's back

- *Bathroom in master bedroom suite.* Not auspicious if located in the wealth or relationship sectors; in this case, always close the toilet cover and the bathroom door after each use; put artificial or real plants in the room, but don't include any cactus

Five

■

BARGAIN HUNTING

Modern department stores have fixed prices, but at open-air markets, souvenir shops, and antique stores, prices are determined by bargaining. There is a myth that it is your persuasive power alone that enables you to bargain down the asking price of a collectible at a dealer's store. Unbeknown to you, the network of dealers in the trade—the invisible hand of the marketplace—have already established a "bottom-floor" price for a collectible, and that price includes both a profit margin and the cost of the product. Feng shui can help you to cut short the haggling time so that the storekeeper quickly agrees to your bid, even though that bid in reality is his "bottom floor" price. The secret is to position oneself inside the store at the "helpful people sector" for easy and smooth bargaining.

For example, in 1962 an authoritative American pocket guide, *Seashells of the World* (Abbott, Golden Press, 1962), identified a cone shell called glory-of-the-seas (*Conus gloria-maris*) as the most valuable shell in the world, a perfect specimen selling at that time for

$1,200.[1] It was prized for its beauty and scarcity. Then shell merchants began to send divers to scour the best shelling grounds in the world—the Philippines. The supply rose to meet demand. Decades later a collector knocked off a dealer's asking price of $25 to $12.50— about 1 percent of the 1962 price for perfect specimens. This collector spotted the glory-of-the-seas specimens under a glass showcase located in the "helpful people sector" of the store. Both customer and seller hovered over the showcase without sitting down at a table. The storekeeper herself picked the best specimen from the inventory, and after less than five minutes' negotiation, she sold it at half the asking price.

In contrast, at another shell store, a lesser quality specimen was on display next to the manager's desk that was situated in the power position—catty-corner to the door. With his back to the door, the buyer sat facing the manager at her desk. The bargaining went nowhere as the manager stuck to her asking price of $25.

Bargain hunting is not barging naively into a dealer's store in search of a collectible. The thrill of the hunt is finding that collectible while positioning yourself in the "helpful people sector" of the store. From there, you conduct win-win negotiations standing up. Before long, your bid will be accepted. (See Fig. 7.)

Not all bargain hunting is designed to knock down prices. Consider the modern charity auction that seeks to raise funds for a worthy cause in the community. It usually takes place at the spacious home of a benefactor. Well-to-do guests gather at this house for a catered dinner, musical entertainment, and an auction of valuable items donated by wealthy patrons. The organizers' aim is to conduct the auction with highly competitive bidders, in order to bring in as much money as possible for their charity and at the same time make the bidder feel that he or she had purchased the item at or

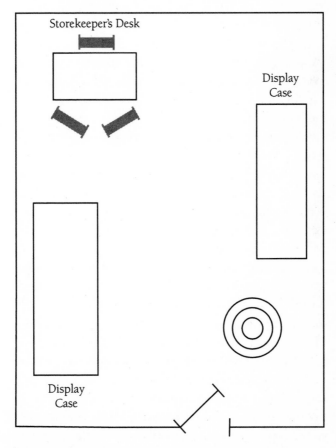

Figure 7. The bull's eye marks the bargain hunter's most advantageous position.

below the market price. The feng shui advice to the fund-raiser is to position the auctioneer in the "wealth sector" of this house, so that the bidding will heat up to a competitive frenzy. Don't let the auctioneer stand in the "helpful people sector" or he or she will sell a valuable item prematurely, and thus at a lower price.

Horse Trading in Teheran

A family vacation in Iran led to old-fashioned horse trading at a fashionable carpet store. In late summer of 1968, Teheran was idyllic; our family of four stayed at a luxury hotel on the hill with a view of snow-covered mountains. Below us beckoned downtown Teheran, where we eventually went shopping. We wanted to buy a Persian rug, a perennial status symbol, to take home on the plane to America. Our driver-guide took us to a carpet store near the British Embassy. The owner then proceeded to display on the floor medium-sized rugs, one on top of each other. We circled around them in the center of the store—an auspicious spot as it is the "balance" sector in the bagua. When my wife and I finally found the rug we liked, I asked for the price. Instead of replying, the owner surprised me by pointing to what he deemed was a status symbol in my possession: the Seiko automatic wristwatch I was wearing. Until he told me, I did not know I had a bargaining chip literally up my sleeve. At that time, state-of-the-art Seiko watches from Japan were primarily sold at reasonable prices in Southeast Asia to cater to the large American military presence there. Seiko became a hit and a status symbol. I bought my watch in Bangkok for $35 U.S. dollars in 1967. Now it was the opening bid for a Persian rug in the bartering of status symbols. In exchange for the watch, plus an additional sum in U.S. dollars, the owner was willing to give me the rug. In the middle of this bargaining, I discovered that I was holding another bargaining chip. He asked me if I could pay by personal check in U.S. dollars rather than in cash. Now personal checks from foreigners are clearly a nonstarter with most merchants, but it was this bargaining chip that brought down the price of the rug to $140 U.S. dollars on top of the Seiko watch. As previously mentioned, a bargain is a highly subjective judgment by a buyer. In our case, we came away happy with a rug that had been woven for several months as a labor of love by young girls of the nomadic Afshar tribe. Similarly, the seller, putting the Seiko watch on his wrist, beamed like a child with a new toy.

Feng Shui Tip: Negotiate while standing in the tai chi or "balance" sector of a store and watch a win-win situation pop up. If you want a steeper discount, move toward the "helpful people" sector. That's the spot close to the door where you can scoff at the price and threaten to walk away from the deal.

The Internet Bazaar

The Internet has become a bizarre bazaar. Purchasing an item online often presupposes that the buyer had already visited other websites to obtain pricing information from competitors. Comparison shopping is accomplished door-to-door in a real bazaar. But in cyberspace, there are no storefronts to visit, just clicks on the mouse with the cursor pointed to one website and then another. In an Internet auction, there is no sound of an auctioneer's rapid-fire delivery rising above the bidding frenzy; instead, it silently draws a widespread customer base, including many loners. The reclusive and the introverted, who otherwise would avoid live auctions, can now share the excitement of a bidding war in real time while shielded from social anxiety.

As buyers and sellers are no longer eyeball to eyeball, does this mean that they are exempt from feng shui precautions in negotiations related to timing, compatibility, and location? The answer is an emphatic no. On the contrary, they have to be more vigilant in cyberspace than in a real bazaar. Impulse buying is encouraged by the ease of online shopping; there is also too much hype over so-called "perfect competition" in pricing. What the impulsive shopper overlooks is that, for example, the cheapest airline does not always appear in the lineup of airlines on a leading travel website. Such cronyism in the Internet occurs whenever a website (not necessarily for travel) heavily promotes the expensive wares of a producer who had paid it an extra hidden fee. Thus, your own patience and auspicious timing are still key factors in the equation.

In cyberspace, compatibility, or lack of it, between buyer and seller appears to be beyond the influence of feng shui methods. Complete anonymity in an Internet transaction means that the buyer would readily fall victim to random acts of meanness ("miscreant chi") in the form of scams by unscrupulous persons. In the real bazaar, a face-to-face encounter begins with an icebreaker—the buyer could either walk away or get reassured that the transaction would be harmonious. In cyberspace, early detection of a seller's "miscreant chi" is not possible. However, potential disharmony between buyer and seller is signaled by several red flags. These telltale signs include: the seller has no contact phone number, does not reply to e-mail queries, promises to get an item that's not currently in stock, and hides the true location of its website using dotless ISP (Internet Service Provider) addresses. In addition, the buyer is asked to provide financial and personal data including social security number.

One way to guard against an inauspicious transaction on the Internet is to place your personal computer, desktop, or notebook at the commanding position in your home office. Your desk should be catty-corner to the door; your field of vision while keyboarding should encompass this door. Your back should be against a solid wall, not against a window, an open bookcase, or worse, a writing cabinet with a fall-front (a symbolic knife in the back). You should avoid placing your computer under a slanted ceiling or a ceiling with exposed beams and metal ducting with sharp corners.

Feng Shui Tip: Your computer helps elevate personal chi. Place it in a room that allows personal and environmental chi to keep rising smoothly upward. An inauspicious room can depress personal chi leading to imbalance, thereby increasing the person's vulnerability to online scams and computer viruses.

Feng Shui Warning: Don't tempt fate with a risky computer placement. A person with a metal chi signature installed his personal computer in the basement with his back to the furnace. In feng shui, this was an unlucky placement because fire melts metal. This homeowner later suffered a tragic death away from home, with burns over 90 percent of his body, under mysterious circumstances.

Six

■

YOUTH'S UNSTABLE CHI

The teenager in your home looks like an adult, but he or she probably does not have the negotiating skills of an adult. At the family dining table, this young person might come across as a hard negotiator who isn't open to reason. Negotiations with this teenager don't seem to work. Your parental concern can be alleviated by taking a more caring approach and analyzing the youth's chi—the patterning energy on the way to adulthood. You do this analysis first, before attempting to negotiate with your teenager. The objective is to direct the smooth flow of chi through their developing bodies. Let youth speak their minds, but be aware that their chi tends to be unstable. In addition, the brain tissue responsible for planning, insight, and organization—the frontal lobe—only starts to mature at age seventeen to nineteen, according to recent findings in neuroscience.

Master Lin Yun said: "If the chi flows through the hand, then you can write; if the chi flows through your legs and feet, then you can walk; if the chi is able to move your tongue, you can talk; if the chi is able to move your brain, then you can think and be fair-minded." But the unstable chi and the developing brain are an explosive mixture for many young people. Young people today are associated with high rates of crime, drug abuse, alcoholism, suicide, schizophrenia, and general social unrest. Those who have a downward moving chi become self-defeating and suicidal. Others may have a chi that comes out of the mouth before reaching the brain—up to the throat, but no further; therefore, these individuals can't think straight, speak up, and seize the opportunities offered to them.

Master Lin Yun has also identified "porcupine chi" among those petulant young people who are disrespectful of authority, quick to put down peers, and prone to violence. You don't open negotiation with this person. You first call in specialists—from school counselors to mental health professionals, if necessary—to conduct the fact-finding. These third parties are needed to decide the facts, the outcome, and the remedy.

The caring approach of using feng shui seeks to adjust the chi flow in the young person and activate the best chi possible in his or her surroundings. The smooth circulation of chi in the young person is the ideal. It energizes the entire body. The upward flow quickens concentration and insight, and at its highest point imbues the young person with ideals of creativity, intelligence, and self-less service. The person with this gift typically looks at you with constantly moving eyes, the look of a budding genius.

The most appropriate feng shui method for coaxing a youth's potential is to place a sun-moon mirror (double-sided) under the teenager's pillow. For safety purposes, however, it should be placed between the mattress and box spring. The mirror should be properly primed as follows: place the mirror on one side outdoors to collect sunlight for twenty-six hours, from 11:00 A.M. to 1:00 P.M. on the following day. Bring the mirror indoors. Later turn the other side of the mirror to collect moonlight for another twenty-six hours from 11:00 P.M. to 1:00 A.M. This mirror enables chi to flow throughout the body and bring in auspicious chi from the environment.

If an adolescent is depressed, you have to raise the chi upward. The feng shui solution is to install a fish tank in the bedroom and stock it with six black goldfish. The tank generates vitality, and the six goldfish would absorb any negative energy in the room. If all the black goldfish should die sooner than expected, it means that they were doing their job well. It also means that you have to restock the aquarium with similar fish. If this young person continues to be uncommunicative with the family, place nine green plants in the bedroom. The artificial variety will provide easy upkeep. These two secret methods would combine to spur troubled juveniles toward spiritual growth and vitality.

Father's Lively Chi

Some parents tend to relive their own youth in their children's activities, resulting in a bumpy ride for their own chi. Colloquially, they are called pushy parents, because they often dream of their children earning top grades in school or excelling in their chosen sport. In feng shui, they are considered parents with lively chi. After a busy day at work, they go out to watch their kids' soccer game. Such a parent goes to bed tired, but the chi travels out of the body to visit places or meet with friends. When the chi returns and the body wakes, a TV screen in the mind shows a brief instant videotape replay of the chi's nighttime travels and observations. This is the feng shui perspective on dreaming.[1] A parent with lively chi would probably dream about some future challenge facing an offspring, as in this example.

A professional family in Detroit had a bright fifteen-year-old son. This teenager was preparing to leave home for the first time on a youth exchange program with Germany. Initially, the father was not totally per-suaded by his son about the wisdom of spending his junior year at a rigorous German high school, even though he had already studied German. He was still immature, the father thought. But one night, the father had probably had a dream of going to the old country to "see" for himself. When the chi returned from sight-seeing via the autobahns of Western Europe, the body awakened to the humdrum sights and sounds of Detroit freeways. His otherwise lively chi wilted into an oppressed, downward-moving chi. He preferred that his son should stay home, but didn't want him to miss the greater excitement of a German secondary school. Secretly torn by this dilemma, the father succumbed to a nonspecific complaint of "just feeling sick" and consulted a physician. He went to the infirmary where, after extensive lab work failed to diagnose the complaint, a nurse jokingly called his illness the "male child deprivation syndrome." After the son left home, the father recovered from this mysterious illness.

Feng Shui Tip: Overprotecting a bright teen may unbalance your chi. If your chi is lively and goes out of the body at night:

- Let your chi go sightseeing where your teen wants to go; then, if you approve of the location, share in his or her adventures; you'll wake up refreshed

- You'll dream of moving up to a new house for the sake of the children; make sure it is located in a prestigious school district where your teens can attend a high school with very good academic and sports programs

Raising a Daughter's Chi

Most American teenagers can hardly wait to take a driving test and receive a driver's license. However, some parents would use this rite of passage as a bargaining chip to gain a teenager's cooperation. They would deliberately postpone this important teenage milestone until they see improvement in the offspring's academic performance. For example, the father of a sixteen-year-old high school sophomore insisted that she raise her grades from a D to a C average before she could get her license and drive the family car. As she participated in after-hours school activities, her parents had to provide transportation; more often, she rode with peers who drove in their own cars. The problem of poor grades was probably exacerbated by the father-daughter negotiation over her driving the family car. If something had to be balanced, it wasn't the father's wheels, but the daughter's chi. The feng shui recommendation is more compassionate and less confrontational: yes, postpone taking the driving test; at the same time, make some adjustments in the daughter's bedroom.

- A brightly lit study desk should be positioned in the "knowledge" sector and her bed placed so that her head is pointing in the direction of the "offspring" sector

- The usual clutter of a teenage girl's bedroom should be removed; place a green rug on the floor to enhance spiritual growth and vitality

- Hang in the "helpful people and friends" sector a small metallic chime with five cylinders

These adjustments should encourage her to spend more time studying at home rather than meeting with friends at the shopping mall. In addition, her teachers and more studious classmates could probably tutor her informally in their spare time so that she could earn passing grades in difficult subjects.

Signs of Chi Balance

How can a parent tell that the teenager's chi had been balanced? Some obvious clues include a clear tone of voice and rosy tinge in the skin. Other signs are subtle. Suppose this hypothetical teenager is an underachieving student with a metal chi signature. In feng shui, a person with an optimum metal chi has the potential to be a good communicator and tends to harmonize with water and metallic objects in the environment. What to look for:

■ In school, the teenager's grades in English should improve sufficiently to be above average

■ In sports, the teenager might excel in swimming competition (metal enriches water)

■ For hobbies, the female teenager might turn to making her own jewelry or dressmaking, using her mother's sewing machine; the male teenager might collect rare coins, build model airplanes, or tinker with cars

In short, the teenager should appear less alienated and experience more harmony at home and with friends at school. Above all, he or she gradually acquires a stable identity based on a supportive network and serene surroundings.

Seven

■

NEGOTIATING FOR A CAR

For most Americans, the most familiar—and most dreaded—negotiation is probably the one that takes place at a car dealership. You are the target of enticing advertisements to visit a showroom. After you have selected the kind of car you want to buy, you do your homework by comparison shopping. However, to be successful, you should include a comparative look at the feng shui of the dealer's showroom where your negotiation will take place. It should be auspicious for a win-win deal that results in your not ending up with a costly lemon. You should first check out the placement of the dealership, using the five animal formulae to describe the lay of the land.

In feng shui, any building and its immediate surroundings form a menagerie of five animals. Each animal represents environmental chi idealized by humans. The building in question becomes the snake, a commander-in-chief ready to strike decisively after coordinating with the input from the other four animals. The dragon on the left side symbolizes vitality and wisdom; the tiger on the right side depicts a vigilant guardian against surprises; the phoenix in front represents a capacity to plan ahead, to innovate and to generate excitement; the tortoise denotes freedom from attack from the rear. This configuration allows you to draw a map on the TV screen in your mind for interpreting whether the place you are about to enter is lucky or unlucky.

Car Dealership Map

The earth has many guises. In modern Tyson's Corner, Virginia, buildings would substitute for mountains and roads for rivers. Since every feng shui method is basically a study of the movement of energy and how to tap this power from the earth, a positive earth chi is discernible as it swirls around an auspicious car dealership (see Fig. 8). A distinctive one-story red brick building, it is the snake in the formula. In the back is a tortoise or mountain: a twenty-four-story hotel in bagua design, protecting it from the cold northwest wind. It overlooks a phoenix river (four-lane Route 7). The curving water dragon (Dulles access and toll road) embraces it on the far left, and a crouching tiger hill (two-story office building) appears nearby on the right.

This classic feng shui configuration in a cityscape should give you some reassurance. The tortoise symbolizes the manufacturer's solid backing for the dealership; the phoenix stands for the excitement promised by the car model; the water dragon adds to your energy and wisdom, and the tiger protects you and your pocketbook. Overall, you get the impression that, with its smooth chi circulation, the place is resistant to urban blight.

(Photo by Air Survey Corporation)

Figure 8. A meandering water dragon is suggested by the Dulles Toll Road interchange with Route 7 in Tyson's Corner, Virginia. The white line encircles the car dealership described in the text.

Watch the Door

Are you then ready to step in with the flow? Not so fast. Check out the main entrance door. If there are two separate entry doors, be prepared for a protracted negotiation. Disagreement and backbiting would prolong the talks. The salesperson would move back and forth, taking longer than necessary to consult with his "closer" or sales manager. If the main door is slanted, take your business somewhere else. A slanted door is a win-lose situation and bad news for you. The customer who goes through it will make an extravagant purchase of a lemon of a car. A worse fate would be for the new car to be stolen by thieves shortly after it is driven away from the dealer's lot.

Fortunately, in this Tyson's Corner showroom, you enter through one main door. It is not slanted. Also, there are no windows. Instead, three sides of the rhomboid-shaped showroom have floor-to-ceiling glass walls. Environmental chi is channeled into an expansive, warm, and welcoming area under two huge crystal chandeliers which disperse positive chi evenly.

Control Freak

Once inside, you have the luxury of only a few minutes to yourself. Instead of admiring the cars on the showroom floor (you have already researched the car you want), use this time to examine the layout of the office cubicles of the sales force—where the chairs and desks are positioned in relation to the cubicle door. Soon a salesperson, a.k.a. Control Freak, greets you politely, and you know which person this Freak would like to control. Don't be him or her. Be on the lookout for any misguided chi. Control Freak's desk and chair are catty-corner to the door, the dominant position. The two chairs for customers back sideways to the door and offer no protection to the car buyer against inauspicious chi. Accept the offer of a beverage, but don't enter the cubicle yet. Ask for a test drive and specify that you want to drive to a nearby county or state park. Conduct your negotiations there. If possible, sit across from the Freak at a picnic table. Let the salesperson use a cell phone to get in touch with the closer. In this way, both of you are uplifted by the high-energy, verdant surroundings. Soon the dealership's price offer will approach your target range. You have a deal. Then go back to the showroom and enter the "control" cubicle to begin the paperwork which the closer, not the Control Freak, should prepare. Your car will then be ordered.

"Antitheft" Options

At some point in your negotiation, you will be asked about ordering an antitheft device for your car. As this is a costly option, the dealership stands to maximize profit at your expense. Ordering it seems a win-lose situation. In feng shui, "antitheft" means countering bad chi in your surroundings. In other words, it means avoiding bad luck. Control Freak can't do this for you. State-of-the art antitheft devices seldom deter the professional car thief, the modern scourge of the streets.

The car owner's ignorance is often an accessory to the crime. The media annually identify the top four car makes likely to be stolen in America, as well as the leading cities with high rates of car theft and car jacking. The real risk attached to car make and city was vividly demonstrated in the following episode. A married couple in the Washington, D.C. area drove their compact Japanese car to Capitol Hill to attend a late-morning church wedding. As the husband parked along the street a block away from the church, he noticed another couple drive into the empty parking space in front of him. He then greeted the occupants, who turned out to have driven cross-country just in time for the wedding ceremony. However, their mid-size American car had previously earned top billing in the media as a favorite target of thieves. After the wedding ceremony, the two couples met again in the street, this time fretting about in the empty spot where the out-of-towners had parked their car. A thief had stolen it in broad daylight, passing up the other couple's Japanese make.

Does this mean that you should not venture into these cities, driving in your ill-fated, but prestigious vehicle? Logic would tell you to avoid these cities, but many a driver would assume that ignorance is bliss as they persist in taking high-risk cars into such a city. Feng shui offers one "antitheft" suggestion for these drivers.

Feng shui Tips: Check if your house or apartment has a missing (inverted) corner in the "knowledge and wisdom" sector of the bagua (Fig. 9). If it is missing, you could become just another statistic as you are prone to forget taking basic precautions such as avoiding high crime areas, or worse, leaving the car keys in the car with the engine running. To correct the missing sector:

■ For a house, plant green bushes as a symbolic completion of the corner

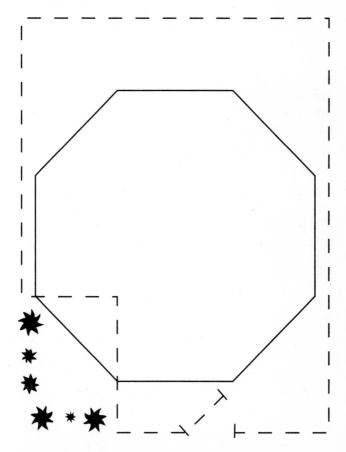

Figure 9. A missing (inverted) corner in the knowledge and wisdom sector of a house can be remedied by planting shrubs to complete or fill out that corner.

■ In an apartment, install a large mirror on the wall by the entrance to give the illusion of depth in the "knowledge" corner, and to protect the premises from theft (Fig. 10)

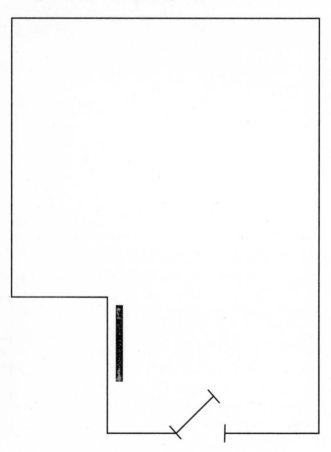

Figure 10. An antitheft mirror next to your home's entrance, restores the knowledge/wisdom sector and protects your belongings from theft.

On the other hand, if that sector is already present in your dwelling, you can be confident in buying the best car you can afford without even ordering an "anti-theft" device.

Used-Car Shopping

In some American cities, a used-car shopper could visit three types of places: a private seller's home, a dealership, and a car superstore boasting no-haggle prices. Before making any visit, the wise shopper checks used-car listings and newspaper ads. Indeed, a local newspaper ad brings the shopper and private seller together for one-on-one negotiation. You begin with a test drive, perhaps with a mechanic friend by your side. This is a proper mundane approach. However, using feng shui, your screening should start with asking for the registered owners. Notice if the co-owner spouse, who is conducting the sale, has another flashy, late-model car in the driveway. Then ask about the other spouse's whereabouts. If this spouse is separated, in prison, or dead, you walk away, even if the price is cheap. You don't want to turn on the ignition every morning and share the ride with the lingering negative chi of the departed or separated owner. This negative chi could adversely affect your own chi, manifesting itself in road rage.

Suppose you have found a registered owner who is anxious to sell. As you want to negotiate the price down, first ask the person to take you to a nearby park or beach. The vibrant chi from the tall trees or body of water would be your ally when *mano a mano* with this private seller. Don't accept the invitation to step into the seller's house for the negotiation. As pointed out elsewhere, there are "lucky sectors" in the house to give the owner an edge in bargaining. You don't want to paint yourself into such a corner.

The feng shui tips for visiting a used-car dealership are the same as those for the new car dealership, described previously. Perhaps you and the salesperson would be sitting across a small desk adjacent to a glass window in the open showroom. The closer or sales manager sits at a desk in a "lucky" spot. You would counter this by negotiating during the test drive outside of the dealership. You should bring along the used-car listings for dogged negotiation. On the other hand, shopping at a car superstore may cut out negotiation entirely, but, contrary to its come-on ads, it may not be a "stress-free" experience for you. After you take possession of the car, you may be sharing the drive with the previous owner's bad karma.

Eight

■

BLESSINGS
THAT WORK

Blessing a Contract Negotiation

The day after you've identified the car you want to purchase, you awaken to the breaking news about the threat of a nationwide auto workers' strike. As a part of the rhythm of American life, negotiations are conducted every three years or so between the United Auto Workers (UAW) union and the Big Three car manufacturers. It's just your luck that the first round of negotiation in Detroit involves your dream car's manufacturer and the UAW. Instead of becoming discouraged upon hearing the news, you turn to a secret feng shui method to unite you with your dream car. You can help the negotiators—at a distance—to reach an agreement by employing the method of visualization that uses the bagua. In essence, you are blessing their efforts to prevent a strike, thus ensuring your car's delivery on schedule. You even can make travel plans in your new car.

Exercise No. 3

The Chi Viewpoint

You relax, meditate, and enter into the spiritual chi state. In this "out-of-body" state, the chi will be able to see whatever it wants to see. It's like a remote viewing experiment. In one such study, a subject in Menlo Park, California, was instructed to move his viewpoint anywhere in the world. When given the coordinates chosen by outsiders, not by the experimenter, the subject described in clear detail the layout of the buildings and nearby equipment on one small island of the Kerguelen Islands, a French possession in the Indian Ocean. He also drew a map of the island.[1] In that experiment as well as in this exercise, the chi is in control, like the creative writer doing his or her best work. Setting, protagonist, and problem flash clearly on that TV screen in your mind which seeks a resolution. The logo in the corner—the bagua—serves as your guide.

When you superimpose this bagua on the map of the United States, Washington, D.C., is the center and the northwest direction, in traditional feng shui, represents the "travel luck" sector (Fig. 11). Detroit, the nation's automobile capital, lies in the northwest direction from Washington. Holding negotiations there is auspicious. The first step is to visualize the presence of a long conference table—not an unlucky rectangular one, but an oval one. The chairs should have good supporting backs and substantial arm rests. You are imaging a bargaining session between the UAW team and the car company team. Each team leader sits catty-corner to the door on the opposite wall. No team leader sits with his back to the door. During a break in the bargaining session, you visualize the UAW president holding a one-on-one discussion with the car company's CEO, with both men sitting on red upholstered easy chairs in bagua formation to elevate the chi and facilitate an agreement. Since negotiation will be prolonged and proper rest will be needed, you imagine

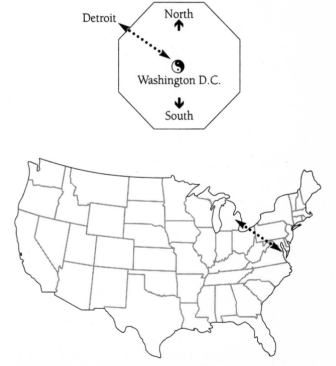

Figure 11. Map of the United States. Bagua directions in the U.S. help to move the chi viewpoint.

an auspicious placement of the negotiators' beds at their homes or in their hotel rooms. The UAW leader's bed is positioned in the bagua sector for "family life" that will be happy, rewarding, and peaceful. The UAW contract proposal had focused on workers' job security, gains in wages, pension, and health care benefits and on tuition assistance for their children. On the other hand, the CEO's bed is located in the sector of "business growth." In each case, the bed is placed catty-corner to the door. This guided imagery using the mystical bagua is the basic design to enhance the negotiators' power and wisdom. If this reality should correspond in some way to the imagery, so much the better. While talks go on, your car is delivered just in time to take you to your out-of-town destination. It is a bonus for you to learn weeks later that a comprehensive agreement is reached and then ratified by the autoworkers. A strike was averted, so you see that your blessing did count after all.

CEO's Chi

In Exercise No. 3, your chi traveled to help "rearrange" furniture at a distance. Most likely, the CEO detected the presence of your chi and, accordingly, harmonized with its good intentions. Business executives, more so than others, tend to be sensitive to hunches, intuitive wisdom, and so-called "paranormal inputs" in making business decisions. The successful ones, as measured by corporate profits over a five-year period, possessed these unusual sensitivities when assessed by objective testing.[2]

A CEO's chi is often lively and active. It directs the delicate balancing act between toughness and tenderness which is expected in a strong leader. For example, the CEO of an Asian communication conglomerate tailored his corporate seminars to stress the spiritual chi state in order that his junior executives become effective negotiators like him. As a young executive, he had attended a training session where a participant was told to grasp a wooden object. This carved wood gradually heated up and burned while held in his tight grip. Apparently, bodily chi, when combined with the wood's chi, created that "spontaneous combustion." This experience convinced the CEO to consider "chi power" before every business negotiation. You send your chi to the office of your counterpart anywhere in the world, and imagine him or her acting and thinking in a reasonable manner toward an issue yet to be discussed.

Negotiating with Gatekeepers

Rarely do we actually hobnob, much less negotiate, with nabobs in America and elsewhere. This section seeks to bring you down to earth with feng shui lessons on negotiating with ordinary persons called "gatekeepers." In the real-life examples that follow, a cross-section of American citizens was involved: males, females, whites, African-Americans, and Asian Americans. The gatekeeper's job requires making quick decisions to allow or deny you access to a place or to a desirable resource. A person occupying this position generally enforces a rule for everyone to follow. However, when the gatekeeper has to make a difficult call, he or she may grant you access only if you negotiate in good faith.

Dress for Access

In feng shui, a wedding ceremony is typically an auspicious event because the bride and groom are positioned to collect blessings (positive chi) from all directions. But instead of hoarding this rich chi for themselves, the newlyweds would in turn spread good luck, a chi adjustment, among the guests. This happened at the conclusion of a church wedding in McLean, Virginia. The bride's younger brother took two passengers—a visiting aunt and the maid of honor—to the wedding reception at a country club in nearby Reston by driving the family car on the Dulles Toll Road. In dressing up for the church ceremony, the women had chosen slim purses specially matching their dresses and left their wallets behind in their rooms. The driver had only the operator's license in the pocket of his tuxedo. When the car exited the toll road, they discovered that no one had any money. The female tollgate collector probably empathized with these members of the wedding party, who were appropriately dressed but highly embarrassed over their predicament. Their nonverbal message to the collector was: "Please don't delay the wedding!" In response, she raised the barrier and let their car pass.

Feng Shui Tip: Nonverbal communication is more effective than excuses in dealing with gatekeepers. Their empathy can be aroused by appropriate dress, by body language, and, most importantly, by chi adjustment following the wedding ceremony.

Hostess of Mercy

What happens when you find out that you are deemed "inappropriately dressed" when you arrive for brunch at an exclusive dining room? You go away hungry, right? The following illustration proved that the influence of the Goddess of Compassion—Kuan Yin—lives on not only in a Taoist temple, but also in an American country club.

An Asian American was invited to a Sunday brunch at a well-known country club in a Washington, D.C., suburb. This visit to an art deco-style country club building, with high ceilings surrounded by murals, reminded him of a temple. Two years before that, he had joined a Taoist temple where Kuan Yin's image shone brightly. As members are often called upon to perform the duties of a lay Taoist priest, they carry for identification a membership card printed with both Chinese characters and English. This plastic card turned out to be the guest's most valuable credential that Sunday. At the dining room entrance, a brunette hostess in a gray suit politely greeted the guest and escorted him to the host's table, located catty-corner to the entrance. Apparently, the hostess had a doubletake about the guest's apparel. Though he wore a double-breasted blue sport jacket and gray slacks, his white shirt with a Nehru collar just didn't pass muster. She returned to the table and whispered something to the host while handing him a gray tie. Then the host turned to his guest and asked him to please put on the tie. Red-faced, the guest went to the men's room to confirm in the mirror how ridiculous it would look to tie a tie around a Nehru collar. On the other hand, storming out and missing a sumptuous buffet brunch was out of the question. In a flash, the bargaining chip appeared in the mirror. A Nehru collar is very much like a priest's collar. "Of course," the Asian American guest said to himself, "I am a lay Taoist priest and I can prove it." He then returned to the hostess at the entrance. In a compassionate manner, he showed her the Taoist temple membership card and explained that the Nehru collar is part of a lay minister's garb. He then offered, as a lay minister, his Sunday blessings to her. She accepted the blessings with enthusiasm and was also greatly relieved at the win-win resolution of the dress code impasse. Most likely, club rules would allow religious leaders in clerical collars to dine as guests at this exclusive club. After enjoying the brunch, the Asian American guest named her the Hostess of Mercy.

Feng Shui Tip: Don't get angry with gatekeepers. Instead, rebalance your own chi by saying a blessing mantra such as "Om Ma Ni Pad Me Hum."

Sexagenarian Disarms Security Guard

The Washington metropolitan area is the nation's center of image making. Images of power seekers are carefully nurtured and protected. Media advisors arrange in advance photo opportunities so that a candidate's personal appearance with ordinary citizens will project the image of a leader with the common touch. The surroundings where the political candidate is photographed also carry a strong message, such as concern for rural poverty or urban gridlock. In this image-conscious environment, a photo shoot using some suburban architectural landmark is probably restricted. If the images are intended for advertising purposes, a written release from the building owners, plus payment of a fee, is required. For example, the Main Street of a well-known planned community in Northern Virginia boasts a large multi-tiered fountain with water cascading into a reflecting pool. A photo shoot by a professional photographer with a well-dressed, sexagenarian client used this fountain as backdrop. Soon it drew the attention of a security guard patrolling the area. The security guard advised the photographer that if the shoot was for an advertisement, he must have permission first from the community association. When told that it was for family purposes, he remained suspicious.

The sexagenarian, sitting poolside, then chimed in. He informed the security guard that he had reached sixty years of age—crunch time in the Asian tradition. At this stage, he explained to the guard, you measure yourself—whether or not you have done the right things along the way. Only a positive balance sheet of merits and demerits would take you farther along. Therefore, it is an occasion for having a professional portrait done and for a family celebration. The sexagenarian then asked the security guard for his age. "I'm twenty-eight," he replied laughing, "and I still have a long way to go!" As he left, he shook the sexagenarian's hand and offered his congratulations for reaching such a ripe old age.

Feng Shui Tip: Negotiate near an outdoor fountain or an indoor aquarium to elevate the chi. Merit making also raises the chi. The sexagenarian earned merit by teaching the security guard to take care of his karma. The security guard earned merit by allowing the photo shoot to continue.

A Stumped Homeowner

As previously mentioned, the typical American homeowner in the suburbs is destined to be a negotiator. Before moving into a new house, the homeowner has to conduct negotiations with several persons, including his or her spouse, the home sellers, and mortgage lenders. After living in the house for a while, homeowners would have to deal with a gatekeeper in the community—the president of the homeowner's community association. Most homes in the suburbs are part of a community association that takes care of shared amenities such as swimming pools, tennis courts, and common grounds. The president and his board, all elected by the association members, are key decision-makers in the upkeep of the common grounds. They are gatekeepers to be reckoned with, as shown in this example.

When the trunk of a large maple tree standing on common ground developed numerous splits, it became an issue for negotiation between a homeowner and a neighbor who was serving as president of the community association. The ailing maple tree directly threatened the western side of this homeowner's residence. For over a year, the homeowner lobbied the community association through letter writing and personal appeals for the removal of this nearby tree. Finally, the president made the decision to hire a tree doctor to cut down the maple tree. Then a board member in charge of the grounds suggested that the association could save money by not paying for the removal of the stump because it would cost extra to bring in special machinery. The tree was cut down, but the stump remained. The president then informed the homeowner about the board decision not to remove the stump, and offered to plant ivy to cover it up so that it would blend in with the homeowner's green lawn.

In feng shui, a tree stump is a source of killing chi. Although the original maple tree had served in the past to protect the western side of the house from the intense rays of the summer sun, the remaining stump became an irritant. This time, the homeowner tried both logic and feng shui in negotiating with the president. He reminded the president that he and his wife had been paying dues to the association for over twenty years and deserved to see their yard improved instead of being marred by a hazardous stump nearby. The estimated cost of the stump removal was only one-third of the expense in cutting down the tree. The homeowners also tried some feng shui methods. They invited the president to come to their house for negotiation. They determined that the maple tree had indeed been cut down, according to the almanac, on a lucky day in May "for felling trees to change feng shui." Under these conditions, they expected that the president would probably be fair-minded about the stump and have a change of heart ("have his chi raised"). It worked. One day in June, a work crew suddenly appeared with a special machine to grind the stump into fine mulch.

Feng Shui Tip: When you wish to negotiate with a neighbor-gatekeeper, invite the person to your home. Don't negotiate with this person at his house or at a formal group meeting elsewhere because they are not auspicious locations for you. Instead, they are this gatekeeper's "power spots."

Feng Shui Warning: Trees can directly affect the homeowners' chi. Overgrown shrubs flanking the entrance as well as trees directly in front of the entrance or windows tend to inhibit the flow of positive chi. Before cutting down a tree in your own yard, consult an almanac for proper timing. If you cut down a tree in your yard on an inauspicious date, the residents of the home may suffer injury to their limbs, bones, or teeth.

The IRS Gatekeeper

How do you negotiate with the Internal Revenue Service (IRS) at a tax audit? For openers, chi adjustment is the way for both IRS official and taxpayer. Cartoonists often portray a domineering official at a desk, staring at a cowed taxpayer. In real life, the average taxpayer negotiates with the IRS by letter and telephone in a business-like and amiable manner. The IRS has a toll-free number to its "Problem Resolution Office." During this negotiation, a number of time-tested tactics would come into play:

- *Power of the printed word.* Suppose you receive a computer-generated letter indicating that you owe the IRS $200 in additional taxes and penalties due to an error in your latest income tax return; your first reaction is to take the computer printout for gospel; you wisely pay up before the deadline to avoid additional interest and penalties; at the same time, the letter invites you to call or write them if the IRS made this mistake

- *Don't get angry with gatekeepers.* Suppose further that the disputed error turned out to be theirs and not yours; if you filed your return without professional help, then you must contact the IRS on your own initiative; you want your money back; the feng shui tip—"Don't get angry with gatekeepers"—applies here, especially because it means that you don't unbalance your own chi

- *Higher authority.* If you sounded very irritable and disrespectful, the IRS official taking your call would probably refer you to "higher authority"; this negotiation tactic works for the IRS because aggressive taxpayers will typically admit that they have no problem working with higher authority; in negotiation parlance, the caller just becomes another "hot potato" to be referred to someone else

■ *Good Guy/Bad Guy.* On the other hand, if you are
polite, this official may be sympathetic and will
try to help you on the spot; for example, the
official may find out, after a review of your return
and listening to your arguments, that indeed the
IRS made a mistake; however, don't expect him
or her to admit this error to you on the phone;
the "good guy" excuse is that your return can't be
entirely pulled into his or her computer screen;
instead, this official will ask you to submit your
documentation in a letter to the IRS District
Office where you filed your return so that it
could make the proper determination; if they
turn you down, they are the "bad guys";
meanwhile, an internal review will probably
result in an IRS taxpayer advocate's decision to
admit an error, hopefully in your favor, followed
by a computer-generated reply to your letter

Feng Shui Tip: Negotiate carefully with the IRS gatekeeper at the toll-free number for its "Problem Resolution
Office." Before you call this office, you may apply the
Three Secrets (p. 87) to balance *your chi.* When your
call gets through, find out the city and state the gatekeeper is in. Then you may send your chi out of body
to visit and bless this person, to balance *his or her chi.*

Nine

■

SECRET REMEDIES

Killing Chi

In today's Switzerland, a Cold War relic is widely observed. Every homeowner must have access to a private or community bomb shelter to ensure that the occupants could survive a nuclear war. During the Vietnam War, a foreign observer walking through the back streets of Cholon, the Chinese suburb in Saigon, would have noticed an unusual display of civil preparedness—octagonal mirrors placed above the entrance doors of several houses. These were not for protection against Viet Cong small arms fire, a fact that he would later discover.

Like the neutral Swiss, the Cholon homeowner was prepared against a more formidable threat—"killing chi" or in Vietnamese, "*sat ch'u*" (literally, "killing the owner of the house"). But unlike the white mushroom of a nuclear blast, killing chi are invisible energy lines. They emanate from sharply pointed angles of pitched roofs in houses across the street; from telephone poles, lamp posts, and electric power pylons; from sharp corners of adjacent buildings; or from the cross on top of a church. Killing chi (also known as "poison arrows") travel in straight lines so that a house facing a straight road or located at the foot of a bridge would draw these converging lines of inauspicious energy. As a homeowner exposed to these dangerous energy lines, you lose the protection of the Geneva Convention against enemy atrocities. Instead, you deploy an array of secret cures to stay alive.

Boardroom Booby Traps

Negotiation teams typically meet in the boardroom of the host team. In this setting, clear thinking is not assured. The boardroom climate is conducive to "groupthink" in which illusions are shared among team members. For example, the out-group might be stereotyped as too corrupt to warrant genuine attempts to negotiate, while the in-group's inherent morality is unquestioned. The illusion of invulnerability is strongly held by team members. When these symptoms of groupthink fill the air, it is time to look around for feng shui booby traps in the boardroom.

The ceiling treatment is often the culprit. A trendy coffered ceiling with indirect lighting may have sharp edges and corners with killing chi aimed directly at the heads of seated negotiators. There may be a protruding corner in the room that seems to divide rather than move the two teams to an agreement. A sideboard behind the team leader could deprive him or her of spiritual support afforded by a solid straight wall in the back. A long rectangular table is inauspicious. Two or more doors promote deadlock. In short, it's a minefield of "killing chi."

A sensitive mine detector is often the feng shui master who can feel the heavy vibrations of such places with negative energy. It sets off an asthmatic wheezing reaction, if not a headache, in an otherwise fit person. As soon as they enter the room, team members would take direct hits from killing chi, unless the premises are first swept clean with feng shui cures. Mundane cures won't work because the offending structures in the boardroom can't be easily altered. What's feasible is a chi adjustment by which a human spirit is able to transform negative energy into positive.

Exercise No. 4

The Three Secrets

As negotiation team leader, you initiate:

1. *In your mind:* a powerful visualization of your team members "dressing for success," "practicing right speech," and "following right conduct" at the bargaining table. What's right or wrong has been determined beforehand at the caucus. These are the conscious intentions that are uppermost in your own mind.

2. *In your body:* The Expelling Mudra. Have your middle finger and thumb describe a circle in each hand and then flick them in front of you; repeat nine times. This outputs bodily chi that counteracts negative energy; if you have a pesky and loud counterpart, use the Repelling Mudra:

the thumbs and middle fingers touch each other while the rest are curled inward; then hold your hands together and point in this person's direction. Your shoulders should always be relaxed (see Fig. 12, p. 89).

3. *In your speech:* Mantra—"Om Ma Ni Pad Me Hum." This mantra also aids breathing and chi circulation, resonating with environmental chi to neutralize negative energy. Deeply inhale with "Om Ma Ni"; then exhale with "Pad Me Hum."

Feng shui is an energetic system, not a "do-nothing" doctrine. There is no equivalent for the notion in Newtonian physics of a "body at rest." Yet when executing the three secrets—visualization, mudra, and mantra—you might appear as a "body at rest," when in fact you are coordinating mind, body, and spirit to benefit both teams. You are taking charge, camouflaged behind the screen of a notebook computer, while performing the three secrets. Like a martial arts master, you're now on automatic pilot as the chi takes over to execute a powerful martial arts form.

Easy Chair Remedy

In Black Hat Tantric Buddhist feng shui, one's orientation to the door in a room is the key to harmonizing with the environment. It does not matter to what cardinal point the door faces, for each compass direction is associated with its own type of luck. A chair facing south would normally be advantageous for gaining recognition and fame, but if it faces the door directly, it's unlucky. A desk with a chair catty-corner to the

Figure 12.

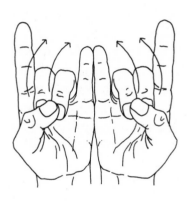

The Repelling Mudra
(Top).

The Expelling Mudra
(Middle). Palms-up
position is for
illustion purposes
only; palms down
position for proper
execution.

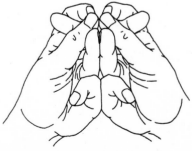

The Blessing Mudra
(Bottom)

door is an auspicious placement, for it gives the occupant the commanding position in the room. This person faces the door diagonally, not directly, to reenergize with the incoming environmental chi. The door symbolizes a mouth that draws in positive cosmic breath. In negotiations, a large conference table is needed to accommodate two parties sitting across from each other, but therein lies a warning.

A long rectangular table tends to be unlucky. It can't be positioned diagonally to the door. In a large meeting room, one team leader takes the power position at the expense of the other team leader who occupies an "unsafe" spot with his or her back to the door. The joint spiritual uplift needed for agreement is not likely to happen. Instead, an adversarial atmosphere builds up. This atmosphere is further poisoned if there are two or more doors, which represent criticism and backbiting, in a large conference room. That's why feng shui-conscious negotiators prefer initially to sit down with the other side in easy chairs in a reception room for informal conversation, before moving on to the plenary session. Later, if the negotiation hits an impasse, they can go back to the easy chairs for a welcome break.

When speaking across the table to his or her counterpart, a negotiator thrusts his or her shoulders forward in the "fight or flight" posture of primates. In martial arts, this position makes a person very highstrung, unsettles the chi, and increases his or her own vulnerability. The obvious solution is to drop the shoulders and not be tense. This posture is made possible during informal conversation while seated in easy chairs with comfortable and firm arm rests. Both parties can drop their shoulders without slumping down on these chairs. Each side becomes less tense, thereby mastering a way to "flow the chi," which could translate into greater persuasive power.

Slants

Feng shui masters have observed over the years that slanted ceilings, beams, and doors have a pernicious ("killing chi") influence on human affairs. The Chinese term for a slanted door is literally the "evil, wicked door." The non-Chinese can also point to horrible catastrophes attributable to the presence of slants. A prosperous businessman was found stabbed to death under the slanted ceiling of his California-style, one-story home, which also boasted dark, exposed beams; the body of his alleged killer, who later died from gunshot wounds, sprawled in the premises. Once, a visitor to San Francisco checked into a hotel near Fisherman's Wharf, where he had advance reservations, and found that the only available room had a slanted door. After spending three nights in that hotel room, he learned in a long-distance call that his mother had died unexpectedly.

The best advice for a negotiator is to avoid occupying a hotel room with a slanted door, but if, like the visitor to Fisherman's Wharf, you are stuck in such a room while negotiating a business deal in town, you can get rid of the negative energy in that room, using the cure described below.

Exercise No. 5

Tracing the Nine Stars

The coordination of visualization and blessing mudra is designed to purify a room of ill fortune and transform negative chi to positive energy.

Begin by connecting the chi energy between your *hara* or *tan den* and hands. Close your eyes and direct attention inward. Let go of any tension in your shoulders, neck, and face. Begin to focus on your breath. Visualize the breath as a stream of energy or white light flowing up your torso from the hara, through your shoulders, down your arms, and out of your fingers.

Visualize the bagua in the room. Use Figure 3 (p. 33) as your mental map. First project your chi and the room's chi from the family sector, to the wealth sector, to the health sector, to the helpful people sector, to the children sector, to the knowledge sector, to the fame sector, to the career sector, and finally to the marriage sector. Then walk the room with the blessing mudra, touching bases with the nine sectors in proper sequence (see Fig. 12, p. 89). You are now in a spiritual chi state—making contact with sources of positive chi while experiencing the negative energy in the room, a painful event in itself. Your job is to bring in positive chi and send blessings to all corners. You transform the pain by visualizing the nurturing presence of loved ones according to the sequence of the "nine stars"—the family star first, through the helpful people star, to the marriage star last.

Chi Compatibility

In every negotiation, the players represent a mix of racial, gender, and individual differences. Every negotiator is unique. Yet to be compatible, all negotiators and their counterparts should share something in common. What commonality exists should be found in their chi. A feng shui secret is to use the "five elements" which are distinctive expressions of human chi. These are "metal," "water," "wood," "fire," and "earth." A person is born with a combination of these elements, but the date of birth in the Chinese lunar calendar determines which element is optimally expressed, so that it becomes the signature of an individual's chi. For example, those born between February 2, 1946, and January 21, 1947, have the "fire" element. Now you have arrived at the intersection between feng shui and Chinese astrology, which categorizes everybody's date and hour of birth according to the elements. Exercise No. 6 (p. 94) shows a method to determine the chi compatibility between any two negotiators.

Exercise No. 6

Method of Determining Compatibility

Step One. Find out the date of birth (DOB) of the principal negotiator and that of the counterpart.

Principal negotiator's DOB: _____(Month/Day/Year)
Counterpart's DOB:_____(Month/Day/Year)

Step Two. Refer to the Appendix to determine the DOB's lunar year equivalent date and its corresponding chi signature.

Chi Signature

Principal negotiator _____
Counterpart _____

Step Three: Do the chi signatures match perfectly? Circle one: Yes No

Step Four: If you circled "No," refer to the "productive cycle" discussed in the Appendix. Do the chi signatures match any one of the five pairings? Circle one: Yes No

Chi Compatibility: If you answered "yes" in Steps Three or Four, the chi of the principal negotiator and counterpart are compatible.

For example, President Ronald Reagan (DOB February 6, 1911) and Soviet General Secretary Mikhail Gorbachev (DOB March 2, 1931) have matching metal chi signatures. Both men were compatible and successfully negotiated the end of the Cold War.

A compatible pair following the "productive cycle" is represented by President Bill Clinton (DOB August

19, 1946), possessor of fire chi, and People's Republic of China President Jiang Zemin (DOB August 17, 1929), an earth chi person. In feng shui, fire produces earth. Thus, when Clinton visited China in June 1998, the two held a well-received press conference on Chinese live television that resulted in raising President Jiang's prestige in China as well as in America.

Sharing an element means having the same optimal chi expression—neither too much nor too little of the particular chi. Though on opposite sides, two negotiators who share an element are likely to produce better agreements than another pair who are mismatched. Compatibility between opposing negotiators is assured if they both have the same element—metal chi, for example.

Food and Negotiation

Feng shui has also something to say about food. First, its adherents favor a traditional diet of soy-based food. Soy lecithin helps lift bodily chi and improve chi circulation. Second, food preparation and presentation are auspicious if they symbolize "chi rising." For example, the role of "wind and water" is key in preparing roasted Peking duck, a standby banquet fare when negotiating in China. Air is blown between the meat and fat so the skin separates from the meat when cooked. The duck is then seasoned and hung so that the dehydrated skin tightens before roasting. The red-gold skin of the finished product is shown to the diners to whet their appetites just before the chef carves it into bite-size

pieces. Each diner then rolls the skin and meat together with julienne scallions and plum sauce, using a thin
pancake. The water theme concludes the dinner with
the serving, say, of shark's fin soup in soy sauce.

Chi expansion is also symbolized in European
recipes featuring souffles, whipped pudding (mousse),
and stuffed chicken breast. Food and beverages are
either chi rising or chi perturbing. Some examples are
discussed in Part II. The table below indicates how certain foods and beverages affected negotiators' chi. Page
references are given.

Chi Rising

Birds' nest soup, p. 128

Soufflé of lobster, p. 171

Hot lemon soufflé, p. 171

Cherry brandy, p. 104

Chinese sugar plum
preserve, p. 104

Cold watermelon, p. 151

Tartar cheesecake, p. 128

Chicken Perigourdin, p. 171

Chi-Perturbing

Roof of hog's mouth, p. 127

Sea snails, p. 127

Samchou (alcoholic herbal
drink), p. 127

Seaweed, p. 127

Airag (fermented mare's
milk), p. 157

Overview

Whenever surroundings suggest the presence of killing chi and negotiators seem deadlocked, these remedies may be useful.

Problem	Remedy
Location: Boardroom's coffered ceiling, protruding corner, etc.	Three Secrets: visualization, mudra, mantra
Location: Large conference table, "fight or flight" posturing	Easy chair cure: placement on commanding spot, shoulders relaxed
Location: Slanted door, slanted ceiling, beams on slanted ceiling	Tracing the Nine Stars: using visualization and the blessing mudra
People: Matching negotiators for a win-win agreement	Method of determining compatibility
People: When chi-perturbing food offered during negotiations	Consume food with chi-rising symbolism

MOVING RIGHT ALONG

From Shirt Sleeve Negotiating to Striped Pants Diplomacy

In Part I, we looked at everyday situations and discussed how the secrets of feng shui could be successfully applied. We used hypothetical examples and real life vignettes that probably hit close to home. You've learned that to attain creature comforts of the good life, one is intuitively negotiating round the clock without realizing it. Moving to a better neighborhood, getting a rare collectible, and taming your teenager to become a thoughtful adult—these are rising expectations that will propel you to consider feng shui for useful tips. At the same time, we disclosed a feng shui secret about what to do in a negotiation if you are meeting at a location not of your choosing—say, the counterpart's unlucky boardroom or an automobile salesperson's cubicle.

In Part II we will consider actual historical episodes in which feng shui had a crucial role. We could have used examples from the business world or domestic politics, but we chose the diplomatic world because the players were often household names. Their successes and failures create high drama, and you can relate to some of the players because you admire them as real heroes. But, as in a Greek drama, some of your heroes would succumb to a blinding hubris, unable to recognize bad feng shui. The lessons learned in these incidents may be directly applicable to your own life situation. For example, what historians considered "lucky breaks" in negotiation between the Emperor of Japan and General MacArthur early in the U.S.'s occupation of Japan were actually the happy confluence of location, compatibility, and timing. From the perspective of good feng shui, you must take care that these three factors are favorable whenever you negotiate.

Part Two

THE UNSEEN DIPLOMATIC PLAYER: FENG SHUI

Ten

■

HOW CHINA LOST
HONG KONG

Overview

- *Players:* The expansionist British brought isolationist China to the negotiation table during the Opium War (1839–42); negotiators were Sir Henry Pottinger and Imperial Commissioner Ch'i-Ying

- *Location:* Nanking

- *Chi Compatibility:* Undetermined

- *Timing:* Random

- *Dates:* Hostilities began June 1840 and ended August 1842

- *Negotiated Outcome:* Zero-sum agreement in which the British won and China lost; China agreed to open up five treaty ports, cede Hong Kong Island in perpetuity, and pay a war indemnity; opium trafficking by British traders continued

■ *Bottom line:* Nanking had bad feng shui without the protective tortoise

Sugar Plums

The Opium War broke out in 1840 when China rejected talks with the world's superpower, Britain. British traders had been illegally selling India-grown opium to the Chinese to pay for their imports of tea, silk and porcelain; widespread addiction posed so serious a national security threat that China banned, at one point, all British traders from doing any business there. While China vigorously rebuffed diplomatic negotiation, she was at the same time totally unprepared for gunboat diplomacy. The China coast soon came under fire from guns of British warships and from commando raids by seaborne troops—3,600 Scottish and Irish Infantry, augmented by British Indian Army units. When Chinese authorities finally sat down for talks in Nanking, British naval guns were pointed toward the city for emphasis.

On the Yangtze River aboard the British 74-gun warship *HMS Cornwallis* on August 29, 1842, China's Imperial Commissioner Ch'i-Ying, together with I-li-pu, a fellow commissioner, signed the Treaty of Nanking to end both the Opium War and China's isolationist policy. Britain, represented by Sir Henry Pottinger, had negotiated a commercial treaty opening up trade to four Chinese ports besides Canton, and for good measure, he had taken possession of Hong Kong Island in perpetuity.

The signing also signaled that the Chinese expectation that foreign devils kowtow to the emperor had vanished. The Chinese signatories were forced to treat foreign devils as equals and had to raise a toast to the health of Queen Victoria with cherry brandy.[1] Attempting to salvage national dignity, Ch'i-Ying drew from his Manchurian roots a ritual often triggered by such an exchange of toasts—he asked mustachioed Sir Henry to open his mouth while he deftly shot into it sugar-plum preserves. As Ch'i-Ying explained, it was an old Manchurian custom to build a high degree of mutual trust. It was this kind of confidence building that unified the clans of nomadic tribesmen in Manchuria to emerge as empire builders. Backed by their soldiers' excellent horsemanship and rapid marksmanship with the bow and arrow, one clan, the Aisin-Gioro, emerged on top and founded the Ching dynasty that ruled China and Mongolia from 1644–1911.

Now that they had lost a war to the British, they were forced to negotiate at a place with bad feng shui. Sir Henry had been instructed by London to drop the demand for Hong Kong Island, but since every negotiation is largely determined by the parties across the table, he exercised his own discretion, just as he would later catch Ch'i-Ying's plums with his open mouth. In addition to the cession of Hong Kong, he also wrested from China a war indemnity to the tune of $21,000,000 in Mexican silver dollars, payable by installments over a three-year period. For security, until the last payment was made, the British occupied two islands that guarded access to the treaty ports of

Ningbo and Amoy. British warships withdrew from Nanking only after they were loaded with silver destined for the treasury in London. Seemingly an auspicious location near a body of water which symbolized money coming in, Nanking by the Yangtze meant money flowing out.

To retrace the steps of the negotiators at Nanking, you have to first walk through the place at different periods of its history. Nanking was a favorite target of conquering warlords and foreign warships. It was the city where the Aisin-Gioro clan's warriors defeated the last holdouts among ethnic Han Chinese pretenders to the Ming throne. It was built by the first Ming emperor Hongwu (literally, "Vast Military Prowess"), a peasant leader who had defeated the occupying Mongols known as the Yuan dynasty. He, in fact, employed feng shui masters to draw up the plan for his Imperial City.

Design of an Imperial City

The master plan was developed by using a checklist of what constitutes good feng shui:

- The feng shui master prepared a mystical map to read the chi of the landscape and the interplay of dynamic forces there; he used a *lopan*—the feng shui compass to be described in the next chapter; he surveyed the landscape to locate various mountains and hills, guided by the five animal formulae

- Starting with the direction he was facing, he identified a snake in the center where he stood;

then he searched for a dragon on its left, a tiger
on the right, a phoenix in front, and a tortoise
behind; these five animals symbolized the
positive chi emitted when mountains were
present in this configuration

■ Facing south, the feng shui master oriented
the proposed site for the Ming palace as the
command center—the snake—with the dragon
in the East (Purple Mountain), the tiger in the
West (a green hill), and the phoenix in the South
(a smaller mountain); however, the tortoise in
the North was missing; there was no protective
mountain in the back; instead the Yangtze River
dominated the northern approach

■ The emperor located the Ming Palace in such a
way that the Purple Mountain would become the
protective tortoise at due north; he also tried to
rectify the missing tortoise for the larger city by
building a red sandstone wall (30 kilometers in
circumference, 36 feet high and 21 feet wide at
the top) to protect the city; the wall had thirteen
Ming gates to provide access to the city

■ Last, but not least, the emperor directed his feng
shui master early in his reign to pick the location
of his tomb; when he died at the age of seventy-
one, he was buried at the chosen spot east of
Nanking, on a slight rise halfway up Purple
Mountain, where a small stream flowed on its
way around the mountain; the mile-long path
leading to the tomb meandered upward to deflect
killing chi, which travel only in straight lines;
for extra protection, rows of large carved stone

animals, soldiers, and bureaucrats were arranged in double pairs along the path so that one set would always be "on duty" around the clock

Nanking's Bad Feng Shui

The emperor's son, upon his accession to the throne, decided to abandon Nanking as his capital. By the time of the Opium War in 1840, a man-made canal connected the Yangtze to a western Ming gate, and water flowed through the walled city and exited at an eastern Ming gate. It was constructed like a scythe cutting into the underbelly of Nanking. The powerful energy of the water placed Nanking in the direct line of fire from negative forces. Moving through this canal, British warships were able to place the whole city within range of their guns. While British forces were planning to move northward to attack Beijing, Ch'i-Ying was appointed Tartar General of Canton, with orders to meet with force British incursions in the south. On the way, he decided to reconnoiter Central China and observe the deployment of the British expeditionary force up the Yangtze River. He was dismayed to learn that the British were using the mile-wide river as an open lane for their fleet to control the Yangtze valley. Nanking and other cities along the "Great River" lay within striking range.[2]

Interestingly, even though they had been the inventors of gunpowder and firecrackers, the Chinese had no reliable shore batteries to deter enemy fleet movements. In the hands of garrison troops, according to a British writer, a Chinese cannon had been a "noisy piece of magic—a bang intended to terrify."[3] In the Opium War, it did what it was "intended" to do—unbalancing the chi of friend and foe alike, nothing else. The British noted how, when their warships approached, Chinese soldiers, after firing the first round, abandoned their cannons and ran.

Beijing's Feng Shui Defense

At this point, what helped save Beijing from a full-scale British invasion was that Beijing had more advantageous feng shui than Nanking. A British ship-of-the-line was a multilevel wooden platform transporting seventy-four heavy guns and crew; therefore, its wooden bottom needed deep waters to clear the sandbar at the mouth of a large river. From recent soundings, they estimated that if they entered the Hai River—the direct lane to Beijing via the Grand Canal—most of their fleet could not cross the bar. Without the fire support from naval guns along these waterways, British commanders would not dare deploy infantry on the plains to cross paths with Mongol cavalry defending Beijing.

Thus, the power of the water dragon in feng shui came to Beijing's defense, for the Hai River and the Grand Canal on the Chinese map were on the dragon (left) side of the south-facing throne in the Forbidden City. In addition, there was Prospect Hill at the back of the Forbidden City—a man-made hill built to rise as a protective tortoise on the dusty plains of Beijing. The Chinese believed that these formidable feng shui defenses at that time forced British commanders to go west up the Yangtze to Nanking, instead of moving north to Beijing.

Ch'i-Ying's Foreign Policy

This foreign threat was countered by Ch'i-Ying's policy of conciliation and realism—"soothing the barbarian"—which was endorsed by the emperor. So the Chinese sued for peace. The barbarians were British forces landing from invading warships that quickly overpowered Chinese defenders. Soothing them was the appropriate remedy in light of China's lack of military preparedness. Ch'i-Ying and the Ching emperor, both Manchurians, were themselves regarded by their Han Chinese subjects as foreigners who were extremely clannish and snobbish. In cities all over China, these foreigners built segregated neighborhoods called Tartar settlements and frowned on intermarriage with the Han Chinese. The last Ching emperor, Pu-Yi, who was educated under a British tutor, said that he identified more with Europeans, Americans, and Japanese than with his own subjects. He later confessed to his Chinese Communist jailers that "during the previous forty years, I had forgotten that I too was Chinese," a people he considered less intelligent than the "white races."[4] Thus, Manchurians could empathize with the barbarians in negotiations, whereas Han Chinese negotiators would only provoke them into open warfare.

Indeed, Ch'i-Ying was seen by the British and later by the Americans as a paragon of reason, etiquette, and spontaneity. China's foreign policy of conciliation and realism during this period reflected his elite origin. A sixtyish Manchurian, he had a friendly face with a wispy mustache and beard. He was tall and portly, with a patrician bearing. He was also an imperial clansman, a descendant of Nurhachi (1583–1615), the founder of the Ching dynasty, and he grew up as a companion of Min Ning, who ascended the throne in 1820 as Emperor Tao Kuang. He had *guanxi*—connections. He served the emperor as personal minister, confidante, and troubleshooter. Nevertheless, Nanking's bad feng shui—the absence of the protective tortoise and the inauspicious canal—forced him to grant excessive concessions to the British. China lost Hong Kong Island at the negotiation table, and it remained a British Crown Colony until July 1, 1997, when a colorful and peaceful hand-over to China occurred.

Eleven

■

DIPLOMACY WITH BARBARIANS

Overview

- *Players:* Triumvirate of Emperor Tao Kuang, Grand Councilor Mu-Chang-A, Imperial Commissioner Ch'i-Ying versus European and American barbarians

- *Location:* Canton

- *Chi Compatibility:* Undetermined

- *Timing:* Determined by the Chinese side

- *Dates:* 1842 to 1850

- *Negotiated Outcome:* Win-win solutions. Commercial treaties signed; excluded were demands for travel of foreign missionaries into the interior and foreign diplomatic presence in Beijing

- *Bottom line:* Canton had good feng shui for diplomacy as it lies in the fame and recognition sector of the bagua

Chinese Self Image

For the Chinese elite, to negotiate was to tarnish their own self-image. They considered themselves culturally superior to all barbarians. Inferiors, whether barbarian or Chinese, were expected to kowtow nine times in their presence.

At this time, diplomacy was contrary to Chinese bureaucratic tradition. Before the Treaty of Nanking, bureaucrats did not officially conduct foreign relations for China. Typically, they let the Canton merchant guild take over the business of "foreign relations" between China and those naval powers from Europe and America that sought to expand trade.

Though China had organized the world's first large-scale bureaucracy through recruitment by competitive examination, foreign affairs as a career path did not exist. The bureaucratic culture embraced a conservative and highly "sinocentric" world-view, with an unabashed sense of superiority.[1] Negotiation with outside powers was unthinkable and unwelcome. "Tribute embassies" from such countries as Korea, Burma, and Vietnam would arrive annually in Beijing bringing gifts, reinforcing the Chinese emperor's supremacy over these dependent states. Some tributes were special orders. For example, in A.D. 1408, the sickly, forty-ish Ming emperor Yongle ("Lasting Joy") sent to Korea the eunuch Huang Yan to screen and bring home as tributes three hundred beautiful young virgins to reside at the imperial harem in the Forbidden City. The emperor was following Taoist prescriptions for life extension and sexual rejuvenation with the help of a vassal state.[2] In such a mission, there was no room for official negotiation or "foreign relations."

Feng Shui in Diplomacy

However, there was a foreign affairs team employed at two bureaus in Beijing—the Board of Rites and the Court of Dependencies. The team was responsible for ensuring that visiting foreign dignitaries observed Imperial Court protocol. They chose the auspicious time for their presentation to the emperor, dictated the court uniform to be worn at the ceremony and coached them to perform the required nine kowtows. The team often sought the advice of an elite group of bureaucrats from the Office of Astronomy and History—the feng shui masters.

Now that China was defeated by the world's superpower, Britain, the emperor himself had to consult these feng shui masters to select the auspicious place for the conduct of diplomacy with Europeans and Americans. The bureaucratic role of feng shui masters was not only to provide advice on policy matters, but also to assist in operations when needed. For example, when the Ming emperor Yongle organized a fleet of warships to explore the Middle East, the fleet commander had on board one feng shui master with four student assistants. Their duties were to conduct astronomical observations for navigation purposes, to engage in weather forecasting, and to advise the fleet commander on auspicious times for shore visits.[3]

Detector of Favorable Chi

The compass was invented by, of all people, the traditional landlubber Chinese. Called *lopan*, it pointed south. It was primarily used as a reliable detector of chi emitted from surrounding mountains, valleys, and rivers. This compass was surrounded by a series of concentric rings; between the rings were calligraphy and numbers. Its inspiration was the bagua, an octagon divided into segments, denoting the eight life aspirations.

In traditional feng shui, each segment corresponds to one of the eight compass directions, which in turn is associated with one of eight Chinese values. The segments and their corresponding luck are as follows: Southeast (wealth and prosperity); South (recognition and fame); Southwest (marriage prospects and marital happiness); West (luck in having children); Northwest (presence of helpful people, benefactors, travel); North (career prospects, business growth); Northeast (education and scholarly pursuits); and East (family relationships).

The values embedded in the bagua made sense to the pragmatic and self-sufficient Chinese, but would have been faulted by Europeans and Americans as ethnocentric. These foreigners risked their lives to travel to China, expressing national drives for exploration and novelty seeking, for trade expansion, for power projection with a strong navy, and for the propagation of the Faith. These social values did not loom large in Chinese officialdom which was mainly focused on tax collection and border control. But now the emperor had to select the location of diplomacy and the venue for a contest of values.

When superimposed on the map of All-under-Heaven (the Chinese Empire), the bagua indicated various auspicious sectors from the perspective of the Ching Emperor sitting in the Forbidden City. The Southeast meant the resource-rich Yangtze delta and the handicraft and trade center of Shanghai. North meant the homeland of the Ching—Manchuria—that insured career luck in the form of dynastic rule and succession. Northwest meant benefactors and allies like the Mongols, whose cavalry protected Beijing. South meant Canton, the communication center for the spread of Chinese culture to the outside world.

Canton was confirmed as an auspicious site for diplomacy. The Emperor created the office of "Imperial Commissioner in Charge of Barbarian Affairs," to be held concurrently by the Canton Governor General. Through this office, he micromanaged official contacts with European states and the United States. Now he had the location and also timely communication. He paid special attention to "oceanic border affairs." Previously, when a border crisis developed, mainly with the Northwest interior, an Imperial Commissioner would be sent to the field as the emperor's troubleshooter, reporting to him directly in written "memorials." This time, however, memorials from Canton could be prepared regularly and could be in the emperor's hands through the official postal system after twenty days.

Chi Compatibility

The emperor had to consider the compatibility factor in negotiation with foreigners. His knowledge about foreigners was derived from political reporting by local officials at the treaty ports. At first, there were three major stereotypes of foreign devil, based on perceived skin color and motivation. The white devils were the Portuguese, "who are fond of women." The red devils were the British and Dutch—so-called because of their ruddy complexion and "slightly yellow hair"— "who are fond of money." The black devils were the Indian Sikhs and Parsees, "who are fond of wine." Later, when Americans arrived in greater numbers, they were called flowery flag devils, a fourth category not based on perceived skin color because the group included whites and blacks (free blacks were among American traders and ship crews seen in Canton). The Chinese were told that allegiance to the United States flag was the defining rule for being an American. They mistook the white stars to be flower petals on the "stars-and-stripes," and the slur "flowery flag devils" stuck.[4]

Personal observation tended to reinforce the concept of foreign devils. One imperial commissioner made an official visit to Macao and was met by the Portuguese Governor General. Carried aloft in a sedan chair with eight bearers, this high official reviewed the honor guard of one hundred Portuguese soldiers in standard-issue European uniforms. Later he wrote about them: ". . . the bodies of the men are tightly encased from head to toe. They look like actors playing the part of foxes. They have heavy beards, much of which they shave, leaving only one curly tuft. Indeed, they do really look like devils."[5]

Most Americans and Europeans who went to China were traders and missionaries. American traders would typically arrive in their clipper ships with a cargo of furs, U.S.-grown ginseng, and Hawaiian camphor wood to sell to the Chinese. They wore dark clothing—thick suits, high collars, stovepipe hats, and boots—and were generally larger than the Chinese buyers. Tall, intimidating sellers in dark suits tended to frighten the very short buyers. While these Americans thought they were "dressed for success," the Chinese believed they were "dressed for stress." The American image thus fitted the foreign devil stereotype.

Chinese officials boasted about negotiating with Europeans and Americans by using a martial arts maneuver of yielding to control an adversary. For example, a memorial to the emperor stated: "[Our] management of barbarians has consisted of taming them by catering to their moods. If the barbarian mood was avaricious, we feigned indifference to money; if the barbarian mood was proud, we treated them with deference; if the barbarian mood was crafty (with) a false front of sincerity, then we showed trust in them. Therefore, for more than ten years there has been mutual accord, and no trouble."[6]

The emperor's foreign policy, as carried out by a conciliatory Ch'i-Ying in Canton until 1848, improved China's standing with outside powers. China signed treaties with the United States (1844), France (1844), and Sweden-Norway (1847). Tension with the British superpower was kept in check. The Europeans and Americans would postpone forcing the Chinese to accept such pet projects as trade expansion in the Yangtze, travel into interior provinces for their missionaries, and a foreign diplomatic presence in Beijing. The British insistence that opium be legalized could wait. Diplomacy was successfully conducted in Canton until the emperor's death in 1850 at the age of sixty-eight.

Twelve

■

AMERICANS MEET FENG SHUI

Overview

- *Players:* President John Tyler and Caleb Cushing on the U.S. side, Emperor Tao Kuang and Ch'i-Ying on the Chinese side

- *Location:* Buddhist temple in Portuguese Macao

- *Chi Compatibility:* Undetermined

- *Timing:* Determined by the Chinese side

- *Dates:* February 27, 1844 to July 3, 1844

- *Negotiated outcome:* Win-win solution. China granted U.S. same treaty ports as the British for trade purposes, "most favored nation" treatment and extraterritoriality; U.S. supported China's anti-opium policy

- *Bottom line:* Americans received a chi adjustment in chi-rich surroundings at the right time

Raising the Chi

U.S.-China history is full of examples of specific locations that were a boon or bane to raising the two nations' chi. Indeed, feng shui played a role in the first diplomatic contacts between the countries. For example, in 1844 President John Tyler—through his negotiator on the ground—ensured the success of one foreign policy initiative through negotiation at a high-energy area in Portuguese-ruled Macao. The site? A Buddhist temple on Avenida do Coronel Mesquita, which was not on Chinese soil.

In 1843, Tyler appointed prominent Massachusetts politician Caleb Cushing to lead the first diplomatic mission to China that July with a U.S. Navy flotilla boasting 200 guns. His flagship was the Navy's new steam frigate, *Missouri*, escorted by the frigate *Brandywine*, the sloop-of-war *St. Louis*, and the brig *Perry*. The firepower was impressive.[1]

The Chinese believed that the Americans' arrival on Feb. 27, 1844, announced with a burst of gunshots, unbalanced their chi. Portuguese fort batteries fired a salute as they approached Macao with American guns returning the courtesy. Later they further rattled more chi by firing a salvo in Canton harbor. The governor of Canton saw fit to warn the Imperial Court in Beijing that it could expect heavy firepower if the Americans were allowed to proceed north. Chinese authorities feared that the positive and smooth chi of the realm could be blasted away. On instructions from the Imperial Court, the governor was to "soothe and stop" the

Americans in Macao where the mission waited in vain for clearance to proceed to Beijing.

In Canton, a second incident that unsettled the Chinese chi during that episode was inadvertently created by Cushing. The American envoy had brought a new flagpole, topped by an arrowed weather vane, to be installed at the American consulate. Americans were already known in Canton by the slur "Flowery Flag Devils." The vane on top of the "Flowery Flag," which the Chinese viewed as an American attempt to direct negative energy—thus killing chi—toward them, so angered the Chinese that a riot erupted within the consulate compound. The mob's ire was directed at the weather vane "which shot to all quarters, thereby causing serious impediment to the felicity and good fortune of the land."

Indeed, shifting wind directions—underscored by the darting movements of the weather vane—made every Chinese neighborhood's chi vulnerable to its negative influence. After 200 Chinese soldiers arrived at the U.S. consulate on orders of the governor, Consul Robert Forbes removed the offending arrow, and order was restored.

The Chinese made Cushing wait four months. On June 18, 1844, he met Imperial Commissioner, Ch'i-Ying, who made an official call at the American headquarters in a rented house on Macao. Riding on a sedan chair carried high on the shoulders of bearers, the commissioner was flanked and followed by Tartar troops. Immediately ahead marched a column of ax bearers. Leading this procession was the grand marshal, brandishing a fan—not a sword—to indicate the Imperial Commissioner's high rank. The fan, a Taoist symbol of smooth chi circulation, signaled that the Chinese were ready to begin friendly negotiations.

The hard-driving Cushing carried the title of "American Envoy Extraordinary and Minister Plenipotentiary"—diplospeak for President Tyler's man on the spot. Though he expected to be received at the Imperial Court in Beijing, he was persuaded by Ch'i-Ying to negotiate a treaty at a Buddhist temple in the obscure village of Wangxia, just outside the city wall but within Macao's borders.

Known as the Temple of the Goddess of Compassion Kuan Yin, this auspicious location was greeted with bemused irony by Cushing, who realized that he would negotiate the first U.S.-China treaty without ever setting foot on Chinese soil. The two parties then held discussions in the most sacred inner shrine of the temple. Temple etiquette required that loud voices be toned down and tempers cooled. The Chinese used another tactic that Cushing found humorous. On the pretext of cramped space, they asked the Yankee lawyer to sit on the sacred spot from which a bodhisattva's image had been temporarily removed. Feng shui supposes there was a chi adjustment with Cushing to steer him to an agreement with the Chinese. Their main worry was Cushing's insistence on going to Beijing with his flotilla. They were also alarmed by his demand for a clause in the draft treaty to allow foreign warships to fire their guns upon arrival at a Chinese port. The Chinese promptly rejected this suggestion.

Despite the initial American perception of the Chinese diplomatic behavior as convoluted, noncommittal, and dilatory, substantive negotiations were completed successfully after only two weeks, from June 19 to July 1.

The signing ceremony, set for July 3, 1844, was classic feng shui. Within the temple compound, the Chinese selected a windowless 30-foot by 10-foot room with one door. An elevated platform, with a table catty-corner to the door, was at the far end. Cushing and Ch'i-Ying sat behind this elevated table. Both were tall men with typically patrician looks. The Yankee perspired profusely under his coat and tie, while his counterpart remained cool in a silk dress with a Manchurian elite yellow belt around his waist. Three other senior Chinese negotiators were present. The Americans who attended in formal attire were: Cushing's secretary Fletcher Webster (Secretary of State Daniel Webster's son); two Cantonese-speaking China hands—Dr. Peter Parker, a medical missionary, and Rev. Elijah C. Bridgman; four attachès—John O'Donnell, Robert Mackintosh, John Peters, and George West; and surgeon Dr. Elisha Kane. Two Tartar officers stood by carrying the Imperial Seal of the Great Ching Emperor. In all, at least fifteen people were packed in that windowless room on a hot and humid summer day.

Eight copies of the treaty were laid out on the table, four in English and four in Chinese. The principal negotiators signed the copies, and the Tartars stamped each copy with the Imperial Seal. At the conclusion, the Americans cheered as they rushed to the door. This upbeat reaction confirmed to the Chinese the wisdom of their chosen feng shui tactic—rectangular room, one door, and no windows—to assure consensus.

The selection of July 3, 1844 bore the unmistakable signature of a feng shui master. In the Chinese bureaucracy, his job was to pick an auspicious date for the signing ceremony and diplomatic receptions. He had been informed that the birthday of the United States falls on July 4, U.S. Eastern time. In Macao (thirteen hours ahead) the astrologically precise time would arrive before high noon on July 3.

Without the astrological sophistication of the Chinese side, Cushing was unaware that he was following in the footsteps of John Hancock, the first signer of another historic document on July 4, Philadelphia time. The Americans gave a luncheon banquet for the Chinese at the rented American Legation following the ceremony, offering in effect a July 4th *vin d'honneur* as well. Cushing had invited the American community, including several women residing in the Portuguese colony. The Chinese reciprocated with a banquet in the evening. These events engendered considerable goodwill, as well as culture shock.

As related later to the emperor, Ch'i-Ying's culture shock was the presence of the "barbarian women." He wrote: "Barbarian custom extols women. Whenever there are honored guests they are sure to present the women. For instance, the American barbarian Parker and the French barbarian Lagrènè both brought barbarian women with them. When your Slave (sic) went to the barbarian houses to discuss matters, these barbarian women would suddenly appear to pay their respects. Your Slave was composed and respectful but uncomfortable, while they were greatly honored."[2]

For the Americans, the culture shock began with Ch'i-Ying's invitation for a "repast of fruits and tea." When they arrived at the Temple of the Goddess of Compassion, they were surprised by what Cushing called a "grand diplomatic dinner" awaiting them. They understood at once why their hosts suggested that they take off the jackets of their white summer suits; but they kept their immaculate coats on, except for one young American who rose to the occasion in shirt sleeves. For, upon sitting down, each guest was given a covered wine ewer, brimming with a hot, potent alcoholic drink called *samchou*. Chinese etiquette dictated that in toasting a friend, one must stand up, raise a cup of samchou with both hands, compliment the friend, drink it, and then wave the empty cup bottom up before sitting down. The feng-shui conscious host seated Cushing, the guest of honor, on his left side—the dragon side in the five animal formulae, the place of honor in which the occupant is imbued with the mystical animal's vitality and wisdom. Another feng shui touch was the first course—a serving of fresh fruit whose color, texture, and artistic presentation were intended to moderate the "fire energy" of summer and induce a hearty appetite for the courses to follow.

For four hours, the Americans and their hosts feasted on such delicacies as sea snails, seaweed, and roofs of hogs' mouths, in addition to the familiar fare of turkey, ham, and roast pig. The entire proceeding was punctuated by frequent toasts with samchou. The banquet was brought to a succulent finish with the serving of bird's nest soup. It was an imported gourmet dish intended to uplift the chi. The raw material had been constructed entirely by swifts, layering their thick and gummy saliva to form a nest. Thousands of these nests were cemented with the same gummy substance onto caves in Palawan, Borneo, and Sumatra.

Ironically, the Chinese obtained the nests from American traders who shipped them from Southeast Asia in commercial quantities aboard their clipper ships. What American traders had sold the Chinese, their countrymen were now contemplating with culture shock. But that was not all. According to Chinese banquet etiquette, the host would have offered Cushing throughout the dinner all the fish eyes and fish lips he could eat, delicacies reserved only for the highest-ranking guest. Cushing was lucky in a way because if the banquet had featured Ch'i-Ying's native Manchurian cuisine, he would have eaten not only its famed steak Tartar, but also goat nipples and bear paws. Instead, the host gave him only one Manchurian delicacy—a parting gift of Tartar cheesecakes. In return, Ch'i-Ying received as souvenir from the Americans an engraved portrait of President Tyler.

The Treaty of Wangxia was a foreign policy success for President Tyler. The Americans came home with four treaty ports besides Canton in their pockets—Ningbo, Shanghai, Amoy, and Fuzhou—and introduced the "most favored nation" clause to benefit the U.S. in case of future Chinese concessions to other powers. They also gained "extraterritoriality," the privilege of trying a U.S. citizen accused of a crime on Chinese soil in a U.S. consular court, instead of a Chinese court. The agreement led to a boom in bilateral trade.

Thirteen

■

GOOD-BYE TO GOOD FENG SHUI

Overview

- *Players:* America's President Richard Nixon and Dr. Henry A. Kissinger versus Chinese Communist power elite, Mao Zedong and Zhou Enlai

- *Location:* Beijing, Mao's residence at Zhongnanhai; Diaoyutai, residence for foreign official guests

- *Chi Compatibility:* Nixon, Kissinger, and Mao shared the water chi; Kissinger's water chi was obstructed by Zhou's earth chi

- *Timing:* Random

- *Dates:* July 1971 to February 1972

- *Negotiated Outcomes:* Win-win for Nixon visit to China and Sino-American rapprochement; zero-sum with U.S. unable to get Chinese help in ending the Vietnam war, and China unable to reclaim Taiwan with U.S. cooperation

■ *Bottom line:* Misguided chi in meeting places delayed formal diplomatic relations

The feng shui masters of the Imperial Court were downsized out of the bureaucracy at the close of the Ching dynasty in 1911, and they returned to their familiar lair in the Taoist and Buddhist temples throughout China. Their services were no longer officially sanctioned. When the Communists seized power in 1949, feng shui practitioners and their clients were intimidated, together with adherents of other "feudal superstitions" such as the Buddhists, Taoists, Christians, and Muslims. Yet feng shui still remained in the culture itself as a secular Chinese system of harmonizing with the environment at home, at the work place, and at the negotiating table.

The Chinese Communist leaders, having driven away specialists in "good feng shui," had unwittingly unleashed the destructive energies of "bad feng shui" in their own surroundings. "Bad money in circulation drives away the good" is a truism in economics as well as in feng shui.

Mao's Study

The first diplomatic contacts in Beijing between U.S. National Security Adviser, Dr. Henry Kissinger, and Chairman Mao Zedong disclosed the danger of killing chi in diplomacy. In each of their five meetings, Kissinger's oversized ego was subordinated to that of Mao. Kissinger wrote: "Mao dominated the room—not by the pomp that in most states confers a degree of

Figure 13. Mao Zedong's study. Left to right: Zhou Enlai, Interpreter, Mao Zedong, Richard Nixon, and Henry Kissinger. In this historic meeting, both good and bad feng shui were evident. Good feng shui: baqua formation of the chairs, guest-of-honor sat on the dragon (left) side of the host; chi balance was attempted by drinking tea to replace fluids frequently directed at nearby spittoons. Bad feng shui: killing chi from V-shaped tables, from the open shelves of the surrounding bookcases, and from the door directly behind Nixon's back. Conspicuous by their absence were Secretary of State William Rogers, who was overlooked by Kissinger and missed the meeting, and Winston Lord, who sat near the second spittoon next to Kissinger—his image was later mysteriously cropped from the photo by the White House.

majesty on the leaders, but by exuding in almost tangible form the overwhelming drive to prevail . . . (he) emanated vibrations of strength and power and will."[1] How could a hypercritical, geopolitical thinker stand in awe of an aging guerrilla leader-turned-tyrant suffering from Lou Gehrig's disease? Feng shui had two answers. First, Mao and Kissinger shared the water chi that made them compatible negotiators (Mao was born on December 26, 1893; Kissinger on May 27, 1923 (see Appendix). Second, miscreant chi lurked in the furniture and layout of Mao's study where the meetings took place (Fig. 13). Bookcases stood against all four walls of the medium-sized room. Mao's open bookshelves were symbolic knives cutting down the visitor to size. But the coup de grace was delivered by the furniture placement in the center of the room. Six upholstered easy chairs with brown slipcovers were arranged in a semicircle. The armrests of two adjacent chairs formed an acute angle into which was inserted a coffee table in the shape of an isosceles triangle. There were five such V-shaped tables, all covered with white napkins. A spittoon was on the floor to Mao's right. The visitor's "place of honor" was to Mao's left—the dragon side. He would rise from an easy chair in the middle to greet his visitor. At that moment, from the feng shui perspective, the visitor stepped right into the converging lines of fire—for the V-shaped tables were symbolic arrowheads racing toward the bull's eye. Five times, Kissinger was mercilessly exposed to these killing chi.

The resulting disequilibrium of the Americans' chi was evidenced not only by Kissinger's upstaged ego, as already mentioned, but also by his uncharacteristic gaffes. When the historic moment arrived for the rapprochement between the rabid anticommunist, Richard Nixon, and the staunch anticapitalist Mao Zedong, Kissinger erred by excluding the Secretary of State, William Rogers, from the proceedings in Mao's study.

Despite his reputation as a diplomatic powerhouse, Kissinger confessed that the one luminous thread of American thinking that made him look good to the Chinese leadership was not originated by the Kissinger team. It was actually derived from a State Department planning document for negotiations which concerned

Taiwan, and it was prepared in the 1950s. One major foreign policy objective—getting Chinese help in extricating the U.S. from Vietnam—did not even merit serious consideration from the hosts.

President Nixon, who was exposed for over an hour to the killing chi in Mao's study, would subsequently introduce a proposal in Shanghai for some sort of defensive military alliance with Communist China.[2]

Chi Incompatibility

The negotiations leading to Nixon's visit to China in February 1972 were conducted secretly between Kissinger and Premier Zhou Enlai. Seen in isolation of each other, both men were gifted negotiators. Zhou was born on March 5, 1898, an earth chi person. This element in moderation means a very frank, honest, and dependable individual who is helpful to others. On the other side, Kissinger, as mentioned above, possessed a water chi. Since the water element signifies insight, clear thinking, and effective social contacts, his diplomatic credentials seemed feng shui-correct. However, when these negotiators interacted, the feng shui rule prevailed—earth controls water. Kissinger had wanted to "paper over" differences and to stress commonalities and mutual agreements in the draft communique for Nixon's visit. Zhou countered with a one-hour diatribe against the American draft that he found untruthful and replete with hackneyed formulas.[3] In feng shui terms, earth obstructed water.

Water was the dominant external feature in these talks. The principal venue was Diaoyutai, the residence for official foreign guests, located west of Beijing. This complex of villas, shaded by trees and dotted with ponds, encompassed the old imperial fishing lake. Each villa was sited on a small peninsula that was connected to its neighbor by a bridge. The negotiators held their secret high-level discussions inside Kissinger's villa. They sat in overstuffed chairs and sofas arranged in a quadrangle in the living room. As noted in chapter eight, sitting on easy chairs with firm arm rests relaxes the shoulders and strengthens the chi, but slumping down on overstuffed furniture keeps the shoulders tense and unbalances the chi. At one point, Zhou invited Kissinger for a one-on-one discussion at another villa on the other side of the lake, and then both took a long walk back to Kissinger's villa, meanwhile crossing two bridges. Contrary to conventional wisdom, a bridge does not symbolize rapprochement; in feng shui, a bridge channels killing chi along its narrow path and threatens the houses at both ends. Kissinger's guesthouse, nestled on a peninsula, would be troublesome for achieving consensus. The positive chi in the lake was being dissipated at the head of the point as water parted into two separate smaller ponds. Water being a metaphor for money, the negotiators inside the villa attracted money, but there was nothing to hold money in. There was neither a supportive dragon on the left, nor a protective tiger on the right.

The feng shui of the place seemed to shape the product of this bilateral negotiation—the Shanghai Communiqué of February 27, 1972. The historic document began with an upbeat message on rapprochement, relaxation of tension, and peaceful intentions in the Asia-Pacific region, but then it bristled with irritants due to two opposing social systems and two foreign policies espoused by the U.S. and China. Normal diplomatic relations had to wait seven years later until January 1, 1979.

Mao's Swimming Pool

If Kissinger's villa was a problematic siting for Sino-American negotiations, Mao's house was hazardous to occupant and visitor alike. A careful dissection of Mao's residence revealed the ravages arising from feng shui neglect. At the end of 1966, just as the Cultural Revolution heated up, Mao moved to newly constructed quarters—later described by Kissinger as "simple and unimposing; it could have belonged to a minor functionary."[4] It was a modest addition designed to bring him closer to his favorite spot, an indoor swimming pool originally built for use by high officials. A visitor would enter the south-facing front door under a portico, going through a small reception room that opened into a wide corridor. At the end was the door to Mao's study, a medium-sized room that had a back door to another corridor leading to his bedroom. Adjacent to the bedroom was his rectangular indoor swimming pool, housed under a tin roof.

Mao, called by his people the Great Helmsman, ran China from a "home office" that alternated between the poolside and his bedroom. His power spot was an oversized, specially crafted wooden bed with a wooden "safety" guard protruding four inches high on one side. He often dined alone at his "office desk," a large square table beside his bed. If Chairman Mao had consulted, rather than intimidated, feng shui masters in 1966, he would have received advice regarding his new quarters something like this: "Moving into this house will bring you adulation from the masses and world renown, but you'll die without a friend at your side. Don't live in a house too close to a large rectangular swimming pool at the back. Worse still, the pool's corner is pointing at the house: you may get very sick and suffer from sexual disorders. This body of water to the rear of the house generates deep and dark chi, which when combined with the killing chi from the pool's corner, will overwhelm you. You'll overdose on killing chi. The back of a house should always be protected by the tortoise, the symbol of solidity."

Shortly after Mao emerged victorious against Chiang Kai-shek in 1949, he needed to legitimize his one-party rule among his people. In 1950, he and his officials moved to Zhongnanhai, at the very center of the old imperial grounds. Mao's compound was the library and retreat of Emperor Chien lung (1736–1796). Above the south-facing main gate, a wooden placard was emblazoned with the emperor's own calligraphy, proclaiming the "Garden of Abundant Beneficence." Originally planned by feng shui masters of the Imperial Court, Zhongnanhai became the stage for Mao's performances as an actor to impress influential foreign visitors. He received them at Chien lung's Chrysanthemum Fragrance Study (his quarters until he moved in 1966). He sought to manipulate foreign governments into preparing and revealing contingency plans for a "post-Mao era." In other words, their official China watchers were encouraged by Mao to tip their hand with a succession scenario early enough for his own patient analysis and secret intervention. What was Mao's standard act?

At the age of sixty-seven in 1961, Mao told visiting British Field Marshal Bernard Montgomery that he could die anytime from disease, from drowning, or from an assassin's bullet. He also admitted to having erred in many ways. Later in 1963, he feigned a near-fatal illness with the Soviet Ambassador at his bedside to elicit Soviet foreign policy changes with his impending "demise." For American domestic consumption, he told journalist Edgar Snow in 1965 that he was soon going to meet God; that year he repeated the same message to Andre Malraux, the French Minister of Culture. In September 1972, Japanese Prime Minister Kakuei Tanaka heard Mao speak his well-rehearsed "dying soon" lines. However, on September 10, 1976, at ten minutes past midnight, Chairman Mao, the actor, finally took his last curtain call at the age of eighty-three. No friend or relative was at his deathbed.[5]

Fourteen

■

THE YEAR OF
THE CAT

Overview

- *Players:* America's President Richard Nixon and Dr. Henry A. Kissinger, versus South Vietnam's President Nguyen Van Thieu

- *Location:* Saigon's Independence Palace, a place with bad feng shui

- *Chi Compatibility:* Nixon and Kissinger shared the water chi. Water nourishes wood—Thieu's signature chi

- *Timing:* Random

- *Dates:* 1963 to 1975

- *Negotiated Outcomes:* U.S. troop withdrawals from South Vietnam; Paris Peace Agreement

- *Bottom Line:* Despite the players' chi compatibility, meeting at Thieu's Palace and his timing were inauspicious

It was the Year of the Cat, so it seemed appropriate that a cat-and-mouse game began on October 31, 1963.[1] Several M-113 armored personnel carriers (APCs) revved up their engines at an army base in Bien Hoa, northeast of Saigon. Troops under a South Vietnamese colonel named Nguyen Van Thieu, Commander of the Fifth Division, climbed aboard APCs and other military vehicles, supposedly to hunt Viet Cong guerrillas to the west, between Thu Dau Mot and Tay Ninh. But it was a diversionary ruse designed to catch President Ngo Dinh Diem in the capital by surprise. As soon as they reached Thu Dau Mot, Colonel Thieu turned south and ordered the formation to gather in Saigon under cover of darkness. Their objective was the capture of the palace the next day. However, Diem was a step ahead. Wearing the robes of a Catholic Redemptorist priest for disguise, he and his brother Ngo Dinh Nhu sought refuge at the house of a Chinese businessman, Ma Tuyen, at Doc Phu Thoai Street in the Chinese suburb of Cholon, where they spent the night.

At early dawn on November 1, 1963, Thieu led his troops in attacking the palace, expecting to personally accept Diem's surrender. After a skirmish with the palace guards, his troops found hoards of Scotch whisky, expensive silks, and antiques, but no president. At 8:30 A.M. when Thieu went to headquarters to report that the palace was secure, he learned that Diem and his brother were killed inside an APC, on their way from Cholon to negotiate a surrender with senior coup leaders in Saigon. A senior coup leader, who allegedly gave the order to execute the Diem brothers, later promoted Thieu to the rank of general officer.

Twelve years later, the cycle came to full circle. In the Year of the Cat, 1975, Thieu, the hunter in 1963, was now President Thieu, the prey. Several similarities with the Diem situation emerged. He was the target of assassination by a South Vietnamese military faction; in fact, on April 8, an F-5 jet bombed the palace in an incident that was an eerie echo of the February 1962 bombing by two warplanes during a coup attempt against Diem. Like Diem, he left Saigon in disguise. He boarded the U.S. Air Force four-propeller C-118 aircraft on a secret "black flight" destined for Taiwan on April 25. He carried credentials as special emissary from the Republic of Vietnam to attend the funeral ceremonies for President Chiang Kai-shek, who had died on April 5. Like Diem, he fled to the safety of a Chinese city. Then on April 30, North Vietnamese T-54 tank crews of the 203rd Brigade, 2nd Corps, roared their engines at full throttle, and at 6:00 A.M. drove toward Saigon for the assault on the palace. On arrival, the lead tank smashed into the wrought-iron gate and stopped next to the flagpole on the grounds. A sapper team leader proceeded to raise the North Vietnamese flag on the second flagpole of the palace's balcony at 11:30 A.M., signaling the conquest of South Vietnam. This cat-and-mouse chase had the same ending as the first—the overthrow of a legitimate government by force.

A Palace with Bad Feng Shui

These two events in the Cat cycle were connected through the saga of Nguyen Van Thieu. He had a rendezvous with destiny at a palace with bad feng shui. The vogue in European architecture and city planning had been to lay out a straight elegant avenue leading directly to the grand ceremonial entrance of a palace. The French followed this classical plan when they built Norodom Palace in Saigon as the administrative seat of Cochin China, a part of the Indochinese Union since 1887. Norodom Boulevard led straight to the palace gate. Inside the grounds, the French tricolor flew on a long flagpole. The layout was feng shui at its worst. When the French finally gave up power in Indochina in 1954, General Paul Ely, the commander of French forces, handed over Norodom Palace to President Ngo Dinh Diem, who renamed it Independence Palace. Norodom Boulevard was "Vietnamized" to Thong Nhut Avenue. But the invisible "killing chi" continued to be channeled through the long straight avenue to the front entrance of the palace. After Diem's violent overthrow, coups and countercoups brought short-term tenants to the palace. Under its roof, high-level American officials negotiated with a procession of South Vietnamese leaders, ending with Thieu.

An Astrologer's Prediction

In September 1965, an odd couple seized power. Air Marshal Nguyen Cao Ky was the front man as premier while Major General Thieu was in control behind the scenes as military junta leader, but General Thieu wanted to remain his country's leader through the electoral process.

He entered his candidacy for president in the upcoming 1967 elections. During the campaign, he consulted a Vietnamese astrologer.[2] He was told that he would win the presidency and that he would remain in power for ten years, ending in 1975, shortly after Tet (the lunar New Year), in the Year of the Cat. For extra insurance, the astrologer advised him to adopt a lucky presidential seal at the moment he assumed office. In feng shui, this act was to be a chi-raising initiative aimed at bringing good luck to the nation. As predicted, he won the elections in 1967 and also in 1971. After his first inauguration in late 1967, Thieu adopted a new seal emblazoned with two dragons facing each other and the national flag in the middle. All Presidential proclamations and executive orders were now stamped with it. It followed the astrologer's design concept to improve his luck.

An argument could be made that these results had really been gained by a self-fulfilling prophecy. After all, Thieu had control of the government apparatus in both elections. He could have completely rigged the elections, but he didn't. He received only 35 percent of the vote in 1967 to win the presidency. There were other developments beyond his direct influence, such as Watergate and the U.S. domestic opposition to the war, which left him vulnerable in 1975. Independently, without the astrologer's advice, he picked the unlucky coup date of November 1 as Vietnam National Day. He would begin nationwide celebrations with a Catholic mass at his private chapel inside the palace. Unfortunately, this celebration was based upon death-oriented religious symbolism.

Booby-Trapped Board Room

The feng shui of the palace exacerbated Thieu's suspiciousness and lack of teamwork among the officials of his government. His office was heavily booby-trapped with "killing chi." It was shaped like a cleaver. The presidential chair, at the end of a long conference table, was located in the handle of this cleaver. Seated in this chair, he was bereft of solid wall support because a sideboard was placed behind his back. At the other side of the room, the grouping of easy chairs placed his chair's back against another sideboard. In both in-stances, Thieu's chi was deprived of a straight wall for support. The spiritual backing needed during negotiation could not be counted on. The office had two doors, which reinforced his indecisive style when presented with conflicting options.

However, the most threatening architectural motif was the protruding corner at Thieu's right when seated at the conference table. The "killing chi" emanating from this symbolic knife's edge split the conference participants and transformed them into haggling bureaucrats jealous of their own turf and led by a chief executive paralyzed with indecision. The internal disharmony was aptly described by Thieu's own ambassador to Washington, who frequently attended cabinet meetings in Saigon: "The meeting was a disaster, not unlike the regular inner cabinet sessions that often lasted an entire day without arriving at a single decision. The ministers spent time arguing among themselves. . . . Shaking with fury, Thieu finally put an end to the session himself."[3]

Because of the President's unbalanced chi, most negotiations with his American allies came to grief. For example, Kissinger praised Thieu's negotiating style when they met outside the Palace, but was critical when they negotiated at Thieu's office. In the Midway Island meeting on June 8, 1969, with President Nixon, Kissinger reported that "he conducted himself with assurance; he did not ask for favors. . . . (Thieu) anticipated us by proposing (U.S. troop withdrawal) himself." But three years later in Saigon, on October 22, 1972, Kissinger perceived another Thieu: "(Ambassador) Bunker and I saw Thieu and (his cousin and aide) Nha at 5:00 P.M. as scheduled, for nearly two hours. . . . Thieu, who spoke English fluently, refused to use it. While talking, he frequently burst into tears . . . Nha translated and at the appropriate passages, he too wept."[4]

Thieu saw the war as a zero-sum conflict with Hanoi, and total victory was his goal. On the other hand, the Americans thought that they and the South Vietnamese had entered into win-win negotiation with

Hanoi in Paris to achieve an honorable compromise. However, Hanoi's Politburo looked to 1975 as an opportune time for a strong military offensive against Thieu.

Prophecy Fulfilled

From the perspective of Chinese astrology, 1975 was the Year of the Rabbit, an animal deemed quick, clever, and ambitious, but unlikely to finish what it starts. Under this animal's influence, Thieu was not to complete his second four-year term. Despite his firm grip on the presidency, he succumbed to his astrologer's prophecy on March 14, 1975 (the Ides of March thus sealed his fate). In an ill-timed decision, he ordered troop withdrawals from the besieged cities of Kontum and Pleiku in the Central Highlands. The pursuing North Vietnamese would soon hasten his downfall with a cruel feng shui maneuver. While advancing on Highway One toward Saigon in mid-April, they issued a battlefield communiqué that the graves of Thieu's parents in Phan Rang, south of Cam Ranh Bay, had been demolished. This unbalanced the president's chi because one's chi and subsequent luck are nurtured by the proper placement and care of ancestral graves. Days later, on April 21, he resigned.

For the Vietnamese, it was understandable why two presidents, both Diem and Thieu, were driven out of the palace in the Year of the Cat. Both men were born Rats.

Fifteen

AMERICANS REVISIT FENG SHUI

Overview

- *Players:* United Nations Command Delegation (led by Admiral C. Turner Joy), North Korean General Nam Il, and Chinese General Teng Hua; Dr. Henry A. Kissinger and North Vietnam's Le Duc Tho; U.S. Secretary of State Madeleine K. Albright and Vanchigdorj, Mongolian herdsman

- *Locations:* Kaesong and Panmunjom, Korea; Paris, France; Jargalent Valley, Mongolia

- *Chi Compatibility:* Le Duc Tho's metal chi compatible with Kissinger's water chi; other players' chi signatures cannot be determined

- *Timing:* Random

- *Dates:* 1951 to 1998

- *Negotiated Outcomes:* Korean Armistice Agreement with neither side claiming victory; Paris Peace Agreement with North Vietnam eventually the victor; U.S. support for Mongolian democratization

■ *Bottom line:* Long rectangular tables are unlucky
for peace talks; smaller tables have better
feng shui

Hollywood has illustrated the inauspicious nature of
long rectangular tables in its *Godfather* films. Invariably
the godfather presides over an Italian-American dinner
at a rectangular table where "family" leaders are treated
to a sumptuous meal. They appear to be resolving a
dispute through negotiation. Then the dinner is rudely
interrupted when an unlucky diner loses his
appetite—and his life—as gunfire rakes the table. In
real life, Americans have had much heartburn and few
heartwarming negotiations because of inauspicious
table shapes. As a result, some negotiators now turn to
nontraditional ways such as "transaction golf," followed by a "cocktail napkin written agreement."[1]

The Korean Armistice Negotiation

During the Korean War, General MacArthur led a
counteroffensive very close to China. Mao and Stalin
decided that China should intervene in the war to pull
their chestnuts—the North Koreans—out of the fire.
Chinese "human wave" attacks pushed back the United Nations forces (led by the United States) from the
Yalu River to the 38th parallel. In late June 1951 both
sides were ready for truce talks. The Americans suggested to the Chinese commander that a meeting take
place aboard a Danish hospital ship in Wonsan harbor, seemingly a neutral location, but the Chinese saw
the hospital ship as bad feng shui. The symbolism of

death and dying was unacceptable. They counter-offered with the old imperial city of Kaesong, then under their control.

Kaesong was once the seat of a unified Korea under the Koryo dynasty, and it also produced the best ginseng in the country, a sign of positive chi. To Chinese amazement, the Americans accepted the location, thus assuring that the Chinese military would be the hosts. An inn at Kaesong, called the "House of Ginseng," was the venue chosen for the talks that began on July 8, 1951.

When the first American negotiators flew in by helicopter, they acted as though they intended to destabilize the talks even before they started. The Chinese invited this liaison team to first sit down in the reception room to break the ice with informal conversation over tea. The American response was clearly insulting to the hosts when they rejected these courtesies. Then they hurried to the adjoining room where a rectangular table awaited them. With a little knowledge of feng shui learned from British China hands, the Americans deliberately sought to unbalance rather than uplift the Chinese and their very own chi. Without waiting for a signal from the hosts, they immediately seated themselves at the side of the table where the chairs faced south. They believed that they had taken the commanding position in the room.[2]

At noon, the Americans refused the offer of Chinese food and instead reached for their own brown bag lunches. After the lunch break, they also passed up a Chinese offer of cold watermelon. It was during this meeting that the Americans rejected the Chinese offer to provide all the food and supplies for the duration of the armistice talks. Thus, the chance for Americans to eat well during negotiations had vanished.

When the two delegations finally began negotiating at Kaesong, the bad feng shui associated with long rectangular tables was soon apparent. North Korean General Nam Il sat on a high chair across from Admiral Joy, who was assigned a lower chair facing north. In one meeting, the North Korean general was obsessed with talking about the 38th parallel as a demarcation line. Because Admiral Joy chose to disregard the subject, the two delegations faced each other across the table in frozen silence—for two hours and ten minutes. In contrast, during a nonplenary meeting, four associate negotiators from both sides sat around a small table and discussed substantive issues in a relaxed and less adversarial atmosphere.[3]

However, an American proposal to move the talks from Kaesong to Panmunjom was accepted by the Communists on October 7, 1951. According to Ambassador Arthur Dean, an official negotiator, "a worse place for peaceful negotiations could not have been found. There was no way in which the normal tensions of difficult diplomatic negotiations could be relieved, and no way in which private negotiations or suggestions could be carried out."[4] Translated into feng shui, Dean knew that Panmunjom had only an inauspicious long rectangular table and that there was no adjoining reception room with easy chairs for purposes of strengthening the chi of both parties while they were seated for informal conversations. The talks were now held under a tent, a far cry from Kaesong's "House of Ginseng." In all, it took two years of negotiation in 160 plenary sessions before the Korean Armistice Agreement was finally signed on July 27, 1953.

Vietnam Peace Negotiations

The shape of the table at another American-initiated peace negotiation spoke more loudly than words, and was heard around the world. In November 1968, during the transition in the U.S. from the Johnson to the Nixon administration, North Vietnamese Communists responded to peace overtures by offering to negotiate with the allies at a square table. The Communists believed that this was not a bilateral (two-party) but multilateral negotiation with equal status accorded to four parties—Hanoi, the National Liberation Front (NLF), the United States, and its ally, Saigon. Negotiating at a four-sided table was intended by Hanoi to breathe life into its progeny, the NLF.[5] Privately they expected to reap negotiation dividends because a square is an auspicious shape. Saigon resisted Hanoi's proposed table, as it would have legitimized the NLF as an occupation force in South Vietnamese territory. The deadlock over the square table lasted for three months until another Communist power, the Soviet Union, intervened with a feng shui solution. The Soviet Union picked an auspicious shape—a circular table. It also stipulated that no nameplates, flags, or markings would identify the negotiators around the table. Everyone concurred. It saved face for the Communists who pretended that the talks were multilateral instead of the bilateral negotiation it really was—the Allies versus the Communists. So on January 16, 1969, the Paris peace talks finally began.

Shortly thereafter, the Vietnamese top negotiator and Politburo member, Le Duc Tho, secretly met for the first time with his American opposite number, Dr. Henry Kissinger, in Paris on February 21, 1970. He promptly unbalanced the chi of the Americans. Kissinger intuitively sensed the bad feng shui around the "dingy, lower middle-class" two-story house on 11 Rue Darthé in the working-class district of Choisy-le-Roi. The door opened onto a small living room adjoining an even smaller dining room, which in turn opened onto a garden. At this meeting, North Vietnamese negotiators took the commanding position in the living room by sitting lined up against the wall cattycorner to the main door. The four Americans sat on the left of the door alongside the opposite wall. They were all seated on red-upholstered easy chairs. Overall the scale of the house's interior was oppressive to the participants' chi.[6]

Almost a year and a half later, on June 26, 1971, a second secret meeting took place, hosted again by the North Vietnamese at 11 Rue Darthé. This time, however, formal negotiation was signaled when the two teams went to the tiny dining room. There they sat at a square conference table covered with a green tablecloth. The green color was an auspicious selection because it conveyed a sense of vitality and positive transformations. However, the two doors in the dining room—one opening from the garden and the other connecting to the living room—seemed to guarantee chronic disagreement. This deadlock was prolonged as the Paris talks resumed in a small conference room at the Center for International Conferences on Avenue Kléber, where the negotiators sat at a long rectangular table. In all, 174 plenary sessions were held there since 1968, with no signs of success despite the chi compatibility between Le Duc Tho's metal and Kissinger's water chi. However, metal has a controlling influence on water. Thus, toward the end of the Paris talks with Le Duc Tho, Kissinger angrily told his own recalcitrant team: "I want to meet their terms. I want to reach an agreement. I want to end this war before the election. It can be done, and it will be done."[7] Kissinger accepted "their terms" which allowed regular North Vietnamese combat forces to be prepositioned in forest areas controlled by the Viet Cong guerillas throughout South Vietnam.

The Paris Peace Agreement was signed on January 23, 1973. Two years later the North Vietnamese finally launched their Great Spring Offensive and overran the South by May 1975. The Politburo boasted afterward that their winning strategy was achieved by this deployment of prepositioned troops that could attack key cities in the South. They called it the "method of cutting down the tree at the roots in order to trap the mice."

Mongolian Tent Meeting

Decades later, America's top diplomat, Secretary of State Madeleine K. Albright, made international news during a spring 1998 visit to the tent (locally called *ger*) of a Mongol herdsman. She had an appointment to meet with a Communist-turned-capitalist and to discover firsthand how Mongolian life—and luck—fared in a free market economy. She encountered instead an informal feng shui practitioner in the person of the host, Vanchigdorj. She entered the south-facing door of the host's tent, which was made of woolen felt stretched across a squat, cylindrical framework of wooden struts. Following feng shui protocol, she was segregated from the men by moving in a clockwise direction to the east (the feminine sector). This sector symbolizes "family relationship." The men stood in the western side (the masculine sector), symbolizing "luck in having children."

This is the traditional placement of the sexes according to the bagua. Despite years of Communist rule, Mongolian herdsmen continue to manipulate their destiny, using the bagua as did their illustrious ancestors. Khublai Khan, for one, had built the fabled Xanadu (Shang-tu) based on feng shui principles.[8] A walled Outer City was designed as a perfect square with sides corresponding to the four cardinal points of the compass. Like boxes within boxes, a walled Imperial City contained the inner walls of the Palace City compound, where in each of eight corners was built a large Buddhist monastery, to correspond to the eight "luck sectors" of the bagua.

Secretary Albright might have noticed the furniture's placement inside the ger: beds, cupboard, and chests were arranged in bagua formation against the wall. The wall was decorated with the Dalai Lama's picture. The herdsman's wife attended to a boiling pot on an iron stove beside the center pole of the tent, which was vented through a hole in the roof. The center of the bagua denoted balanced chi; indeed the dairy delicacies heated on the stove were intended to promote both harmony and health.

The Secretary of State sat on a stool by a small table laden with generous servings of *airag*, the national drink made of fermented mare's milk. "Delicious," she was quoted as saying, "This is the yogurt that makes you live forever." In response to her query about the new regime, the host indicated that life had improved now that he had freedom to raise as much livestock as he wanted. And this diplomatic encounter, held at a small square table, was deemed a success.[9]

Sixteen

AMERICAN
POWER SPOT

Overview

- *Players:* General Douglas MacArthur and Emperor Hirohito of Japan

- *Location:* U.S. Embassy, Tokyo, Japan

- *Chi Compatibility:* The general's earth chi harmonized with the emperor's metal chi

- *Timing:* Astrologically determined by the Japanese

- *Date:* September 28, 1945

- *Negotiated Outcome:* The emperor admitted responsibility for the Pacific War; MacArthur later wrote that the emperor "played a major role in the spiritual regeneration of Japan," thus assuring a successful allied occupation[1]

- *Bottom line:* Chi compatibility, easy chair remedy and auspicious timing led to close cooperation between the general and the emperor

The Search for a Power Spot

Like Chinese emperors, America's leaders have received guidance from feng shui masters on ways to concentrate their power. The advice has been right on the money.

- Before President Ronald Reagan readjusted his view of the Evil Empire in 1983, Master Lin Yun advised him to move his desk forward four to five inches because he was sitting with his back too close to the wall: "This will not only improve his reputation and power—help his chi rise—but also will widen his perspective, opening his mind to new ways to solve the nation's problems," *The Washington Post* reported[2]

- Early in 1997, Time Magazine reported that Master Pun Yin had urged President Clinton to move from the Oval Office to a rectangular one "where straight walls would provide spiritual support and enhance feelings of control"[3]; the feng shui warning, still unheeded, was aimed at safeguarding his chi equilibrium; a month later, the president had a painful misstep while on an out-of-town trip and returned to Washington on a stretcher

The Oval Office has always perplexed feng shui masters. The pumping of chi to an office's interior can be aided by doors and windows, but too many openings—seen as mouths voicing different opinions—can lead to indecision. The best power spot for a desk in an office is catty-corner to the door. Since the Oval

Office has four doors and, of course, no straight walls, the auspicious catty-cornered desk placement in relation to the main door is impossible.

Other locations seemed more fitting than the Oval Office for America's power projection at home and abroad.

Location, Timing and Compatibility

During World War II, despite the widespread fire-bombing of Tokyo, the Americans spared the Imperial Palace, Emperor Hirohito's residence, from air attacks. Uncannily, they foresaw that they would someday meet with the emperor in person. Shortly after Japan's unconditional surrender, the emperor requested a meeting with General Douglas MacArthur. The general indicated that it was inappropriate for him to go to the Imperial Palace and suggested that the venue be the U.S. Embassy where he resided. On the day of the meeting, September 28, 1945, the emperor's departure from the palace grounds was probably astrologically timed at 10:00 A.M., the exact moment when American lookouts spotted the motorcade of black Daimlers crossing the moat outside Sakurada Gate. They then notified the general, who had left his office early to be at home for this important meeting.

He received the younger, nervous emperor at the embassy's drawing room, and they sat down in easy chairs by the fireplace to begin negotiations. The location had good feng shui. And these two antagonists, the general (born January 26, 1880) and the emperor (born April 29, 1901), struck a deal sooner than

expected because MacArthur's earth chi took prece-
dence over Emperor Hirohito's metal chi. In the Appendix (p. 189), the earth element is father to the metal
element. The general's earth chi signature predisposed
him to be frank, honest, and helpful to the emperor. In
turn, the emperor's metal chi led him to do what he
deemed right and to express his thoughts clearly to the
general. The two leaders met for thirty-eight minutes.
The emperor did not know then that MacArthur had
already decided not to try him as a war criminal. In his
opening statement, he took sole responsibility for
Japan's conduct of the war, thus putting himself first in
the lineup of the usual war criminal suspects, but the
emperor did not plea bargain with his admission of
guilt. This meeting left a deep impression on Mac-
Arthur. After that first encounter, they visited each other
twice a year and developed a father-son relationship.
For his part, the emperor rallied his people in support
of the general who led the allied forces' occupation and
rehabilitation of their defeated nation.[4] While the general himself selected the Embassy as the power spot for
the negotiation, the Japanese picked the auspicious timing—between 10:00 A.M and 12:00 noon. Most likely
the emperor's lord privy seal, the Marquis Koichi Kido,
nicknamed "Kido the Clock" by the court staff, chose
the timing of this unprecedented visit from the "Emper-
or of Heaven," but unbeknownst to all, the negotiation
also benefited from chi compatibility between the general and the emperor. The three favorable factors; location, timing, and chi compatibility, all contributed to
the success of this win-win encounter.

Seventeen

■

CHATEAU FLEUR D'EAU

Overview

- *Players:* American President Ronald Reagan and the Soviet Union's General Secretary Mikhail Gorbachev

- *Location:* Versoix, suburb of Geneva, Switzerland

- *Chi Compatibility:* Reagan and Gorbachev shared the metal chi

- *Timing:* Astrologically determined

- *Date:* November 19–21, 1985

- *Negotiated Outcome:* "The most important result of the two-day meeting was that it allowed both leaders to discuss differences in a candid and private setting" (State Department analysis foreshadowing the beginning of the end of the Cold War)

- *Bottom line:* Reagan and Gorbachev had location, timing, and chi compatibility—all favorable

The Golden Glow

In his 1960 nonfiction book *Thrilling Cities*, Ian Fleming, the creator of James Bond, wrote: "Traditionally a haven for refugees from turmoil and persecution, modern Switzerland has gathered to its bosom fugitive royal families, Italian, Romanian, Spanish, and Egyptian, together with a handful of sheiks. These sad orphans of the world's storm, evicted from their palaces, have found shelter in the Palace Hotels along the shores of Lac Leman."[1] It was in Geneva twenty-five years later that the Cold War was suddenly orphaned. When President Reagan met there with General Secretary Gorbachev, neither one claimed to be its parent. Indeed, the Cold War took after the likes of Fleming's royalty—an exile driven away from home by an irresistible force for change. Its name was *glasnost,* or "openness."

President Reagan prepared for the Geneva summit with down-to-earth advice from U.S. officialdom. He was willing to reduce by 50 percent U.S. nuclear arms comparable to Soviet SS-20s and to cooperate in regional peace talks to end armed conflicts in Afghanistan, Cambodia, Angola, Ethiopia, and Nicaragua. Besides security issues, his initiatives included youth and citizen exchanges to upgrade the ongoing cultural and educational exchange program with the Soviet Union. Privately, Reagan geared up for his meetings with Gorbachev with additional help from two sources: astrology and feng shui. The president's briefer was his wife, Nancy, who had spent three hours on the phone with a San Francisco astrologer, Joan Quigley, discussing the upcoming summit. Raising the president's consciousness appeared to be the main theme of that phone conversation. The astrologer warned Nancy that Reagan's "Evil Empire" bias would be disastrous if transported to Geneva: "They'll share a vision. What's more, when Ronnie and Gorbachev meet, they'll get along famously, better than you can imagine if—and this is a very big if—Ronnie goes to Geneva with the proper attitude."[2]

The president was ripe for a change in his attitude toward Gorbachev. Two days before his departure, he was subjected to cross-pressures from Nancy and from the substance of his nationwide address, conciliatory toward the Soviet Union. Soon his private "Evil Empire" beliefs began to crack under the weight of Nancy's persuasion. He kept an open mind about the Soviet leader, consistent with the positive tone of his predeparture address to the nation about the U.S.-Soviet relationship.

The astrologer timed the departure of President and Mrs. Reagan aboard Air Force One from Washington, D.C. at 8:35 A.M. on November 16, 1985, with an eye to enhancing Gorbachev's receptivity to Reagan's message as well as assuring a safe trip to Geneva. However, astrology played only a supporting role. Both men were feng shui compatible, and Geneva was the right place because of its good feng shui. While the seed of glasnost was already planted when Gorbachev's predecessor Andropov occupied the Kremlin, it first sprouted by the waters of Lake Leman.

The chosen venue was a twenty-room, nineteenth-century chateau overlooking Lake Leman in Versoix, a northern suburb of Geneva. Fleur d'Eau is replete with positive feng shui associations. *Eau* is water in French and feng shui in Chinese means "wind and water." The chateau faced southeast, the direction for wealth and prosperity, and occupied a lakefront location. As water equals money in feng shui, wealth was flowing in. Moreover, Fleur d'Eau rhymed with "dough." A bird's-eye view indicated that the chateau was protected from the harsh north winds by the Jura mountains in the back. Symbolically, it enjoyed considerable security, especially freedom from attack from the rear. The summit's location clearly supported the themes to be discussed: arms control and access to the prosperous market economy in the West.

Arriving two days before the talks, President and Mrs. Reagan did what veteran Hollywood stars would do before a shoot—go on a scouting expedition to the set. The couple toured Fleur d'Eau the day before the talks. They entered the meeting room as though both were feng shui practitioners casing, as well as blessing, the premises: "When we walked into the meeting room, Ronnie sat down in his chair, and I impulsively sat in Gorbachev's. Ronnie looked over at me and smiled. 'My, Mr. General Secretary,' he said, 'You're much prettier than I expected.'" From the chateau, they walked to a boathouse a hundred yards away where "we found a beautiful room with a fireplace, and a breathtaking view of the water. Ronnie was eager to meet with Gorbachev privately, without their advisers, and as soon as we walked into the room, we knew it was the perfect spot."[3]

The summit formally opened when the two leaders and their official delegations attended the plenary session at Fleur d'Eau. The conference table had a long ovoid shape. (Fig. 14) The talks went on for two hours, mainly discussing arms control issues. Then the President suggested to Gorbachev that, in his own words, "we go out and get some fresh air and have a little meeting alone. Before I had the sentence finished, he was out of his chair." Both men and their interpreters went to the boathouse that had received

(Photo courtesy Ronald Reagan Library)

Figure 14. U.S. President Ronald Reagan (fourth from left) and U.S.S.R. General Secretary Mikhail Gorbachev (second from right) meet across an ovoid table in Chateau Fleur d'Eau, near Geneva, Switzerland, an auspicious location for talks that led to the end of the Cold War.

(Photo courtesy Ronald Reagan Library)

Figure 15. Reagan and Gorbachev enjoyed a fireside chat in the boathouse at Chateau d'Eau. The furniture was arranged in a bagua formation, suggested earlier by Master Lin Yun.

Nancy's blessings the day before. (Fig. 15) The elder American president had a one-on-one discussion with the younger Soviet leader in front of the fire for one hour and twenty minutes, well beyond the fifteen minutes allotted by the U.S. schedulers. The two men sat in easy chairs arranged in the bagua or octagon formation. Master Lin Yun had suggested this auspicious chair formation to the Reagans in 1983. The feng shui easy chair remedy worked its magic because their shoulders were relaxed, indicating smooth chi circulation. In contrast, some minutes previously, the two leaders had their shoulders hunched in "fight or flight" posture at the negotiation table, mirroring each other's unbalanced chi.

The golden glow of the fireplace touched the shoulders of both men who were born in a metal year—Reagan in 1911 and Gorbachev in 1931. In feng shui, metal is gold, and it symbolizes autumn—the moment of the talks—and stands for the virtue of righteousness. The match was perfect. The person with an optimum metal chi (between too little and too much) is fair, speaks persuasively, and listens well to dissent. When someone expresses an opposing view, he will criticize, but not alienate him or her. Reagan told Gorbachev: "This is a unique situation. Here we are. Two men in a room together. We're the only two in the world who could bring about World War III. At the same time, maybe we're the only two who can bring about world peace."[4]

On another occasion, he said to Gorbachev: "We don't mistrust each other because we're armed. We're armed because we mistrust each other." From November 19 to 21, 1985, the two metal persons had fifteen hours of meetings, including five hours in one-on-one discussions. Reagan found his counterpart a risk-taker and a "remarkable force for change." At the summit's conclusion, he was pleasantly surprised that he "would eventually call Mikhail Gorbachev a friend."[5] Shortly after leaving the White House, Reagan himself rated his meeting with Gorbachev at the boathouse as the "most important moment of his presidency."[6]

For his part, Gorbachev confided when already out of office that it was at the next summit meeting, in

Reykjavik, Iceland, that Reagan finally won his complete trust. Despite the deadlocked ending, they both savored an intense give-and-take discussion across a small rectangular table inside a villa by the sea.[7]

Red Lobster, White Goldfish

In diplomacy, an agreement can be hammered out after several hours at the negotiating table. Feng shui wisdom suggests that also crucial are the precious moments at the dinner table. Good food is not only intended to provide bodily sustenance but also to elevate the human spirit to new heights. The Reagans' feng shui helpers in Geneva came from unexpected quarters—Aga Khan IV, his wife, the Begum Salina, and their young children.

The spiritual leader of the twenty million-strong Nizari Ismaelite Muslim sect, Aga Khan IV is Prince Karim, son of Aly Khan and stepson of the legendary Hollywood star Rita Hayworth. The Harvard-educated prince and the begum lived with their children in an eighteenth-century chateau on Lake Leman called Maison de Saussure. When they learned that the Reagans were coming to Geneva, they offered their home to the President, who graciously accepted the offer. The Prince and his wife moved out, leaving behind the staff and house chef at Mrs. Reagan's disposal. Their children personally entrusted to the leader of the Free World the care and feeding of the goldfish in the residence.

On the second night of the summit, the President and Mrs. Reagan hosted a dinner for Mikhail and

Raisa Gorbachev. Eight other guests from the U.S. and Soviet delegations were present. As described by the hostess, "the house looked wonderful with the fireplaces lit and plenty of flowers all around."[8] The dinner menu consisted of soufflé of lobster, supreme of chicken Périgourdin, endive salad, mousse de fromage with avocado, and for dessert, hot lemon soufflé with raspberry sauce. California wines were served. Gorbachev ate his soufflé dessert with gusto and complimented the hostess effusively because he had never tasted a soufflé before. Her chi-raising initiatives symbolized by the soufflés of lobster and lemon succeeded beyond expectation. She said: "The previous night, when I met Gorbachev for the first time, I felt a certain coldness from him. At our dinner, however, he warmed up considerably. From then on, the more I saw him, the more I liked him."[9]

However, other guests at the dinner party were rather disagreeable persons, but the Aga Khan's residence was equipped with a secret feng shui remedy to cope with such swirling negative energy—an aquarium with goldfish to absorb "killing chi." In America, the goldfish is the second most popular pet, after the cat, suggesting an intuitive appreciation for this feng shui aspirin for the home. Senior officials from both sides who were at the dinner had been busy earlier working on a draft of the joint statement at the summit. U.S. Secretary of State George Shultz then told the president that they were at loggerheads over the language of the final document: "The Soviets wanted to change something that had already been agreed upon."[10] After dinner, the two teams worked late into the night. Meanwhile, the president and his wife retired for the evening and discovered that one goldfish in the aquarium had died. He felt guilty because, as he put it, "it occurred during my watch." He put the dead goldfish in a matchbox and in the morning asked the Secret Service to find a replacement at a Geneva pet store. That day Reagan went to his last televised appearance with Gorbachev with the dead goldfish in his pocket. In fact, television footage of the ceremony disclosed a matchbox-size bulge in Reagan's suit pocket.[11] The goldfish had died in the line of duty, shielding Reagan from the negative energy emitted by the Soviet negotiators. It had been the president's secret feng shui protector.

Eighteen

FRAGRANT HARBOR WATERS

Overview

- *Players:* "Mandarins" at the British Foreign Office and at the Foreign Ministry of the People's Republic of China (British official records will be made public in 2014)

- *Location:* Beijing

- *Chi Compatibility:* Undetermined

- *Timing:* Random

- *Dates:* 1984–1997

- *Negotiated Outcome:* Zero-sum agreement in which the Chinese Communists won (under the terms of the Sino-British Joint Declaration on the Question of Hong Kong, ratified on May 27, 1985, Hong Kong became a Special Administrative Region of the People's Republic of China starting on July 1, 1997)

- *Bottom line:* Hong Kong's chief executive needs a new official mansion to maintain prosperity

If there is a single spot on earth under the micro-
scope of famous feng shui masters, it is Hong Kong
Island, prize of the Opium War. It was initially viewed
in London as a "barren island with hardly a house
upon it." By the time they gave it back to China, the
British Crown Colony was rated the eighth-largest
trading entity on earth. Americans called it then the
freest economy in the world.

Nature's script for Hong Kong's return carried the
feng shui theme—that is, "wind and water." On the
day of the turnover, July 1, 1997, winds buffeted the
territory, and heavy rains caused minor flooding and
landslides. The British were at first reluctant to give up
Hong Kong Island as this was territory ceded to them
in perpetuity by China. But to survive, the island needed water. Most of its water supply came from leased
land in China. After the lease expiration, the Chinese
Communist government could have used this "faucet"
as leverage in any negotiation.

In 1898, however, British negotiators could have
averted Hong Kong's return to China. They were negotiating in Beijing with the weakened Ching dynasty.
They wanted to extend the British Crown Colony
north of Kowloon up to the Shenzen River, and 235
nearby islands. If the British had kept their eyes on the
ball, the strategic question would have been: "How can
we provide Hong Kong with a stable water supply in
perpetuity?" The answer would have been cession to
Britain of the New Territories where water reservoirs
are now located. Instead the British mission in Beijing
cast suspicious eyes north toward their Russian rival

and asked themselves: "How can we thwart Russian territorial ambitions in China?" The answer: To prevent Russia from seeking the cession of Port Arthur (Lushon) in perpetuity, Britain would lead by example and ask the Chinese only for a lease of ninety-nine years for the New Territories and the 235 islands.

The search for the source of Hong Kong's good fortune under British rule would usually begin and end at Government House. This British governor's mansion in ornate classical style was planned in 1851 and completed in 1855. Probably it had the benefit of a feng shui master's advice: it sits in the classic configuration of a chi-rich environment, midway down a mountain range, overlooking the sea.

But a closer look, using the five animal formulae, discloses that Hong Kong was highly vulnerable. Government House is the command center, the symbolic snake coiled and poised to strike. There is a dragon to its left and a phoenix in front. The dragon is Victoria Peak with its spine meandering toward the entrance of the house. The south-facing door sucks in this stream of super-rich chi. The phoenix is framed by the Zoological and Botanical Gardens in the mountain range next to Victoria Peak, but on the right of Government House, there is no vigilant tiger as guardian of this flank—no hill. The protective tortoise in the back appeared later when the Hong Kong and Shanghai Bank building was built below the hill. Within these auspicious surroundings, negotiations conducted in Government House led for a time to win-win agreements.

At the urging of lobby groups, successive governors promoted the flow of goods, money, and information in and out of Hong Kong, with no red tape and minimal taxation. For their part, businessmen honored contracts, and residents cooperated with an administration run by incorruptible civil servants and honest judges.

However, Hong Kong's golden age under British rule peaked in 1984. According to some feng shui masters, at the start of the year, Government House was standing in harm's way. A blade-like structure, the Bank of China skyscraper, towered over the financial district and was poised to slice into Government House. These masters feared that the British governor, Sir Edward Youde, would be at risk. Since assuming office in 1982, he was in the eye of the storm surrounding the status of Hong Kong. He took part in the negotiations between London and Beijing that culminated in the "Sino-British Joint Declaration on the Question of Hong Kong." But this agreement to return Hong Kong to China did not provide for a way to achieve some form of self-rule by Hong Kong residents after 1997. The governor still had to negotiate this fact with the Chinese. While in Beijing in 1986, he suffered a heart attack and died.

His successor, Sir David Wilson, moved into Government House in 1987 fully aware of its bad feng shui. A China scholar on the British Foreign Office team that negotiated the 1984 Joint Declaration, the new governor (born February 14, 1935, and thus a wood chi person) took prudent countermeasures. He wanted to bolster the defense around Government House and stay alive. These cures included:

- Planting soft willow trees to counteract the "killing chi" from the sharp edges of the Bank of China

- Nurturing the azaleas and rhododendrons on the grounds to circulate the positive chi and continuing the custom of one-day public viewing of the flowers in full bloom around March

- Replacing the rectangular swimming pool—and its sharp corners aimed at the mansion—with a round one, a more auspicious shape

- Cutting off water going down the hill from the grounds; it symbolized Hong Kong holding onto its wealth, for *water* in Cantonese slang means *money*; ironically, the water previously going downhill was flowing in the direction of the British-owned Hong Kong Bank, which attracted the lion's share of deposits from Hong Kong's residents

Did these remedies work? Yes, definitely. The governor's wood chi also helped. Wood is the element of benevolence, loyalty, and forgiveness; the bamboo in feng shui symbolizes peace and safety. When hit hard by the global stock market correction in October 1987, Hong Kong rallied shortly thereafter. Street demonstrations erupted in sympathy with the victims of the Tienanmen Square massacre on June 4, 1989, but China's leaders were later accepted if not forgiven. The Basic Law was published in 1990, concluding

Anglo-Chinese negotiations on representative government in Hong Kong after 1997. The colony went back to doing what it did best—making money.

The governor himself successfully warded off serious illness and accidents. Sir David Wilson had a passion for mountaineering, which took him to the far corners of the colony. One day he went hiking in the Pat Sin range in the New Territories, overlooking a large reservoir. Running down a very steep hill, he tripped on a stone, lost his balance, and injured himself. Feng shui masters took dark pleasure in saying, "I told you so." Government House still had bad feng shui. But the governor's luck, according to his wood chi, held out. Wood overpowers earth. When interviewed by a journalist about what part of Hong Kong should be named after him in the future, he replied, "A rock face somewhere."[1] Though the Chinese have yet to carve his likeness on a mountainside, he ended Her Majesty's service in 1992 in good health and was made a baron for life, as Lord Wilson of Tillyorn.

The next and last British governor, Chris Patten, was not so fortunate. For five years, he vigorously worked himself out of a job, persuading Beijing to allow more democratization in Hong Kong. For his efforts, he underwent heart surgery. Then he saw his patron in London, Prime Minister John Major, lose to Tony Blair. On the day of Hong Kong's turnover, Prince Charles and China's President Jiang Zemin officiated at the ceremony, upstaging the governor. That evening Chris Patten bid farewell to the mansion and then sailed away from Victoria Harbor with Prince Charles on the Queen's yacht *Brittania*. In the drizzle, Government House on Upper Albert Road stood silent and abandoned.

The British Governor's successor, C. H. Tung, hand-picked by China, started his first day in office as Hong Kong's Chief Executive by moving into a government building on Lower Albert Road, not in Government House. He positioned himself at a better feng shui location. After a heavy rainfall, the run-off from the American Consulate directly up the hill passes by the chief executive's building as it meanders to the sea. To Chinese eyes, American water (that is, money) has continued to flow into Fragrant Harbor, Hong Kong's Cantonese name. Hong Kong also continues to enjoy a comfortable trade surplus with the United States, its major trading partner.

For his residence, the chief executive selected a third-floor apartment in a high-rise building perched midlevel on a mountainside overlooking Government House and the financial district. But soon after, economic turbulence hit Asia and made waves in Fragrant Harbor. Now a fresh feng shui issue has emerged because some constituents blame this economic downside on a wicked underground open pit inside the chief executive's residence.[2]

Nineteen

■

CONCLUSION: DIPLOMACY FENG SHUI-ED

"Diplomatic negotiation," according to Charles W. Freeman, Jr., veteran American diplomat and author, "is bargaining between states." In his "realist" view of diplomacy, the two major players are (a) the diplomat who acts as agent of his state in other states and (b) the agent's principal, the head of state. The two should exercise a combination of "diplomatic skill and the power and agility of the state they represent, rather than the imposition of principle and precedent, to decide the outcome."[1] However, as suggested by our historical analysis, this "realist" approach overlooks a third player from the total picture—feng shui. Once again the 1985 Geneva summit meeting between President Reagan and General Secretary Gorbachev clearly illuminates these ingredients for diplomatic success. U.S. Secretary of State George Shultz (born December 13, 1920) was an ideal agent at the side of his principal, President Reagan. They were an effective political team, as both men shared the metal chi signature. The main outcome of the meeting—raising the chi of Reagan and Gorbachev—would not have been possible without Shultz's help and the factors of timing, auspicious location, and the chi compatibility between the principals themselves. Thus, a third unseen player was present. The principal negotiators, seemingly on opposite sides, were propelled by good feng shui toward future cooperation. Paradoxically, the "realist" view could no longer overlook this paranormal component.

If the paranormal affected bargaining between rival superpowers in the past, it could also help or hinder diplomatic negotiations now and in the future. For example, President Clinton, a fire chi, had brokered the peace talks between Palestinian Chairman Yasser Arafat (born August 24, 1929) and then Israeli Prime Minister Benjamin Netanyahu (born August 21, 1949). These two principals from the Middle East shared the earth chi signature. Fire, paired with earth, constitutes a parent-child relationship in feng shui. President Clinton, the parent, was expected to settle the two offspring's dispute firmly and peacefully. In brief, the three leaders' chi compatibility helped move the talks forward. After eighteen months of American mediation, in the fall of 1998 the president finally succeeded in getting the Israeli and Palestinian leaders to sign the Wye River Memorandum, so-called because their meetings were held at a rural retreat by the Wye River in Maryland. Under the agreement, the Palestinians received tangible economic benefits, safe passage between the West Bank and Gaza, and the promise of Israeli troop redeployments. In turn, the Israelis won

Palestinian assurances of greater security measures against terrorist attacks and U.S. promises to pay for the security-related costs in implementing this agreement.

(Photo by Jose Armilla)

Figure 16. The dining room of the Wye River Conference Center where the Israeli and Palestinian leaders negotiated a peace agreement, October 1998.

Shortly thereafter, Prime Minister Netanyahu unilaterally postponed implementation of the Wye Agreement and then lost his job to a challenger in the popular vote. What went wrong? When he negotiated with Arafat in the dining room of the Wye River Conference Center, both men were up against bad feng shui. They labored under the influence of an inauspicious ceiling, slanted at a forty-five degree angle, with exposed beams. As we saw earlier, slants and exposed beams tended to attract bad luck. Netanyahu's successor as prime minister was Ehud Barak (born Feb. 12, 1942), a possessor of metal chi. Negotiations between Netanyahu and Arafat could proceed in harmony as metal "comes out" of the earth, but the two should observe the usual caution in picking an auspicious conference room because chi compatibility alone is not enough to produce a win-win outcome.

Look at the arrangements for the peace talks between Arafat and Barak, July 11–25, 2000, at Camp David. The timing was poor. The almanac had indicated a lunar eclipse on Sunday, July 16, 2000—a phenomenon likely to sow distrust of the other side's good faith effort.

The choice of Camp David failed to compensate for the poor timing. Granted, this presidential retreat in Maryland's Catoctin Mountains had a track record: Arab and Israeli talks in September 1978 led to a peace treaty between Israel and Egypt on March 26, 1979. But bad feng shui haunted the negotiators as well as the mediator at that time, President Jimmy Carter.

After the peace agreement, the political careers of the chief players ended abruptly.

In the summer of 2000, Arafat and Barak, together with President Bill Clinton as facilitator, negotiated in sunlit patios and along asphalt walkways in the woods—auspicious settings indeed. At dusk, however, the negotiators sought what they perceived as the coziness of the cottages and lodges at Camp David. Once inside, they fell under the oppressive influence of slanted ceilings and exposed beams—building motifs linked to headaches, heartburn, and foot-dragging when making hard decisions. The peace talks collapsed, ostensibly over the question of who will rule Jerusalem, and the Middle East remained a tinderbox.

Confronting another regional flashpoint, President Clinton's fire chi has posed a threat to Yugoslav President Slobodan Milosevich (born Aug. 20, 1941), a metal chi person, as "fire melts metal." No wonder the two leaders have yet to meet seriously at the negotiating table even after the air campaign against Yugoslavia. But the president's agent, Ambassador Richard Holbrooke (born April 24, 1941) had close and frequent interactions with the Yugoslav leader. As both share the metal chi signature, the American envoy and author had characterized Milosevich as a "smart" and "charming" person.[2] What kept this Serb leader at loggerheads with the U.S. and major European powers? Perhaps it was partly the result of bad feng shui. At Dayton, Ohio, in the fall of 1995, Holbrooke negotiated with other Balkan antagonists at an inauspicious venue—an air force base replete with killing chi. At one plenary meeting, the negotiators sat across a long rectangular table placed directly under the wing of a huge B-2 bomber that was suspended from the ceiling of a hangar. On exhibit nearby hovered a Tomahawk cruise missile, a grim reminder of outside intervention in the Balkans. It was not exactly a chi-raising experience for Milosevich and others.

Political negotiation tends to give belligerents a spiritual uplift, especially when good feng shui is present. Asian warlords in medieval times offered this feng shui lesson on how to turn enemies into loyal supporters. After a bloody invasion, captured officials would be brought for talks at the camp of the victorious commander-in-chief. The camp had the layout of an ancient Chinese city with good feng shui. It was a square enclosed by tamped earthen walls, with the main gate facing south. Intersecting streets, running north to south and east to west, provided for interlocking bands of fire to light up this tent city after dark. In the center, the commander-in-chief's banner flew over the single entrance to his headquarters tent (the symbolic snake). The decorated tents of his advisers stood closely on the dragon side (left), while those of the elite swordsmen of his personal guard encircled the headquarters, providing security on the phoenix side (front), the tiger side (right), and the tortoise side (rear). Scores of lavishly embroidered flags and banners whipped in the wind, decorated with figures of tigers, birds, dragons, snakes, phoenixes, and tortoises. These were unmistakable feng shui enhancements to raise everyone's chi. The rest of the encampment housed soldiers in gers, a feng shui-correct mobile home that had been transported in wagon trains to the camp. Dazzled by the surroundings and impressed by their captor's generosity, some enemy prisoners would then agree to cooperate as civilian administrators of "All-under-Heaven." This medieval image had repercussions in recent U.S.-China diplomatic relations.

After Chinese President Jiang Zemin arrived in the U.S. for a state visit in October 1997, he had a summit meeting with President Clinton and his foreign policy team. Then the Chinese leader found out that the state dinner being prepared in his honor would be held not inside the White House but on the lawn outside— under canvas tents. Diplomatically, he requested his hosts to hold the dinner indoors. Unbeknownst to the Americans, the Chinese probably realized that any television image of their top officials dining inside the tent of a powerful world leader would shock most educated Chinese at home. It was too reminiscent of the Mongol conquest of China. The wily Genghis Khan had co-opted Chinese officialdom by inviting captive officials to negotiate with him under his tent. This fear of being dominated once more by a foreign power seemed to surface during President Jiang's visit. However, President Clinton's accommodating style in negotiation was partly reassuring. Chinese negotiators had expected him to be a friendly and paternalistic counterpart in bargaining. In their political culture, negotiation is often exemplified by a magistrate giving a lecture and sage advice to a petitioner "on the principles" to be observed rather than a decision-making process among equals.[3] As pointed out elsewhere, President Clinton's fire chi had been helpful to President Jiang's earth chi, as fire "creates" earth.

Some European analysts recently questioned America's current esteem for China as a "strategic partner" when it acted more like a strategic foe by targeting its nuclear weapons on the United States.[4] These analysts overlooked the fact that China has played its American card by applying feng shui to negotiations with good results. For example, during President Clinton's stay in Beijing, he occupied a luxurious suite complete with three adjoining whirlpool bathtubs in his bathroom at Diaoyutai Guest House; this feng shui overkill was probably intended to raise his, as well as America's, chi. American negotiators in China have endured banquets featuring chi-rising as well as chi-perturbing cuisine. Then there were those "innocent" side trips to feng shui-correct places such as the Forbidden City and the Ming Tombs. Both sides of the negotiation might be so dazzled by the ambiance as to forget later which country is a paper tiger. This is good feng shui in action: Chinese and Americans would negotiate on thorny issues without saber rattling. Despite its low ranking as a military power, China remains on the diplomatic front burner for America because of the danger of war across the strait of Taiwan.

When regional conflicts heat up, diplomatic negotiation is the preferred way to maintain international order. During an international crisis, democratic leaders routinely ask for political support from the people. Yet, for many, diplomacy remains a mystery. But don't despair. From this book, you have already gained some insights into diplomacy's inner, spiritual workings, because feng shui is the unseen player in bargaining between nations.

Appendix

■

FINDING THE CHI SIGNATURE

The chi signature of a person is determined by the year of birth according to the Chinese lunar calendar. The Chinese New Year begins on the second new moon after the winter solstice. Table 1 (p. 192) shows the Gregorian calendar year, its Chinese lunar year equivalent, and the chi signature associated with the lunar year. As the Gregorian calendar alone does not lead to accurate identification of a person's chi signature, always refer to the lunar year.

Note how yearly progression is accompanied by cyclical change in chi signatures. This change follows the "productive cycle" of the five elements:

- Metal enriches Water (minerals give water its satisfying taste)

- Water nourishes Wood (trees)

- Wood aids Fire

- Fire produces Earth (volcanic eruptions create mountains and islands)

- Earth yields Metal

Table 1. Chi Signatures of Birthdates

Gregorian Calendar Year	Chinese Lunar Year	Chi Signature
1870	31 January 1870–18 February 1871	Metal
1871	19 February 1871–8 February 1872	Metal
1872	9 February 1872–28 January 1873	Water
1873	29 January 1873–16 February 1874	Water
1874	17 February 1874–5 February 1875	Wood
1875	6 February 1875–25 January 1876	Wood
1876	26 January 1876–12 February 1877	Fire
1877	13 February 1877–1 February 1878	Fire
1878	2 February 1878–21 January 1879	Earth
1879	22 January 1879–9 February 1880	Earth
1880	10 February 1880–29 January 1881	Metal
1881	30 January 1881–17 February 1882	Metal
1882	18 February 1882–7 February 1883	Water
1883	8 February 1883–27 January 1884	Water
1884	28 January 1884–14 February 1885	Wood
1885	15 February 1885–3 February 1886	Wood
1886	4 February 1886–23 January 1887	Fire
1887	24 January 1887–11 February 1888	Fire
1888	12 February 1888–30 January 1889	Earth
1889	31 January 1889–20 January 1890	Earth
1890	21 January 1890–8 February 1891	Metal
1891	9 February 1891–29 January 1892	Metal
1892	30 January 1892–16 February 1893	Water
1893	17 February 1893–5 February 1894	Water
1894	6 February 1894–25 January 1895	Wood
1895	26 January 1895–12 February 1896	Wood
1896	13 February 1896–1 February 1897	Fire
1897	2 February 1897–21 January 1898	Fire
1898	22 January 1898–9 February 1899	Earth
1899	10 February 1899–30 January 1900	Earth
1900	31 January 1900–18 February 1901	Metal
1901	19 February 1901–7 February 1902	Metal
1902	8 February 1902–28 January 1903	Water

Table 1, Continued

Gregorian Calendar Year	Chinese Lunar Year	Chi Signature
1903	29 January 1903–15 February 1904	Water
1904	16 February 1904–3 February 1905	Wood
1905	4 February 1905–24 January 1906	Wood
1906	25 January 1906–12 February 1907	Fire
1907	13 February 1907–1 February 1908	Fire
1908	2 February 1908–21 January 1909	Earth
1909	22 January 1909–9 February 1910	Earth
1910	10 February 1910–29 January 1911	Metal
1911	30 January 1911–17 February 1912	Metal
1912	18 February 1912–5 February 1913	Water
1913	6 February 1913–25 January 1914	Water
1914	26 January 1914–13 February 1915	Wood
1915	14 February 1915–2 February 1916	Wood
1916	3 February 1916–22 January 1917	Fire
1917	23 January 1917–10 February 1918	Fire
1918	11 February 1918–31 January 1919	Earth
1919	1 February 1919–19 February 1920	Earth
1920	20 February 1920–7 February 1921	Metal
1921	8 February 1921–27 January 1922	Metal
1922	28 January 1922–15 February 1923	Water
1923	16 February 1923–4 February 1924	Water
1924	5 February 1924–24 January 1925	Wood
1925	25 January 1925–12 February 1926	Wood
1926	13 February 1926–1 February 1927	Fire
1927	2 February 1927–22 January 1928	Fire
1928	23 January 1928–9 February 1929	Earth
1929	10 February 1929–29 January 1930	Earth
1930	30 January 1930–16 February 1931	Metal
1931	17 February 1931–5 February 1932	Metal
1932	6 February 1932–25 January 1933	Water
1933	26 January 1933–13 February 1934	Water
1934	14 February 1934–3 February 1935	Wood
1935	4 February 1935–23 January 1936	Wood

Gregorian Calendar Year	Chinese Lunar Year	Chi Signature
1936	24 January 1936–10 February 1937	Fire
1937	11 February 1937–30 January 1938	Fire
1938	31 January 1938–18 February 1939	Earth
1939	19 February 1939–7 February 1940	Earth
1940	8 February 1940–26 January 1941	Metal
1941	27 January 1941–14 February 1942	Metal
1942	15 February 1942–4 February 1943	Water
1943	5 February 1943–24 January 1944	Water
1944	25 January 1944–12 February 1945	Wood
1945	13 February 1945–1 February 1946	Wood
1946	2 February 1946–21 January 1947	Fire
1947	22 January 1947–9 February 1948	Fire
1948	10 February 1948–28 January 1949	Earth
1949	29 January 1949–16 February 1950	Earth
1950	17 February 1950–5 February 1951	Metal
1951	6 February 1951–26 January 1952	Metal
1952	27 January 1952–13 February 1953	Water
1953	14 February 1953–2 February 1954	Water
1954	3 February 1954–23 January 1955	Wood
1955	24 January 1955–11 February 1956	Wood
1956	12 February 1956–30 January 1957	Fire
1957	31 January 1957–17 February 1958	Fire
1958	18 February 1958–7 February 1959	Earth
1959	8 February 1959–27 January 1960	Earth
1960	28 January 1960–14 February 1961	Metal
1961	15 February 1961–4 February 1962	Metal
1962	5 February 1962–24 January 1963	Water
1963	25 January 1963–12 February 1964	Water
1964	13 February 1964–1 February 1965	Wood
1965	2 February 1965–20 January 1966	Wood
1966	21 January 1966–8 February 1967	Fire
1967	9 February 1967–29 January 1968	Fire
1968	30 January 1968–16 February 1969	Earth
1969	17 February 1969–5 February 1970	Earth

Table 1, Continued

Gregorian Calendar Year	Chinese Lunar Year	Chi Signature
1970	6 February 1970–26 January 1971	Metal
1971	27 January 1971–15 January 1972	Metal
1972	16 January 1972–2 February 1973	Water
1973	3 February 1973–22 January 1974	Water
1974	23 January 1974–10 February 1975	Wood
1975	11 February 1975–30 January 1976	Wood
1976	31 January 1976–17 February 1977	Fire
1977	18 February 1977–6 February 1978	Fire
1978	7 February 1978–27 January 1979	Earth
1979	28 January 1979–15 February 1980	Earth
1980	16 February 1980–4 February 1981	Metal
1981	5 February 1981–24 January 1982	Metal
1982	25 January 1982–12 February 1983	Water
1983	13 February 1983–1 February 1984	Water
1984	2 February 1984–19 February 1985	Wood
1985	20 February 1985–8 February 1986	Wood
1986	9 February 1986–28 January 1987	Fire
1987	29 January 1987–16 February 1988	Fire
1988	17 February 1988–5 February 1989	Earth
1989	6 February 1989–26 January 1990	Earth
1990	27 January 1990–14 February 1991	Metal
1991	15 February 1991–3 February 1992	Metal
1992	4 February 1992–22 January 1992	Water
1993	23 January 1993–9 February 1994	Water
1994	10 February 1994–30 January 1995	Wood
1995	31 January 1995–18 February 1996	Wood
1996	19 February 1996–7 February 1997	Fire
1997	8 February 1997–27 January 1998	Fire
1998	28 January 1998–15 February 1999	Earth
1999	16 February 1999–4 February 2000	Earth
2000	5 February 2000–23 January 2001	Metal
2001	24 January 2001–11 February 2002	Metal
2002	12 February 2002–31 January 2003	Water

Table 1, Continued

Gregorian Calendar Year	Chinese Lunar Year	Chi Signature
2003	1 February 2003–21 January 2004	Water
2004	22 January 2004–8 February 2005	Wood
2005	9 February 2005–28 January 2006	Wood
2006	29 January 2006–17 February 2007	Fire
2007	18 February 2007–6 February 2008	Fire
2008	7 February 2008–25 January 2009	Earth
2009	26 January 2009–13 February 2010	Earth
2010	14 February 2010–2 February 2011	Metal
2011	3 February 2011–22 January 2012	Metal
2012	23 January 2012–9 February 2013	Water
2013	10 February 2013–30 January 2014	Water
2014	31 January 2014–18 February 2015	Wood
2015	19 February 2015–7 February 2016	Wood
2016	8 February 2016–27 January 2017	Fire
2017	28 January 2017–15 February 2018	Fire
2018	16 February 2018–4 February 2019	Earth
2019	5 February 2019–24 January 2020	Earth
2020	25 January 2020–11 February 2021	Metal
2021	12 February 2021–31 January 2022	Metal
2022	1 February 2022–21 January 2023	Water
2023	22 January 2023–9 February 2024	Water
2024	10 February 2024–28 January 2025	Wood
2025	29 January 2025–16 February 2026	Wood
2026	17 February 2026–5 February 2027	Fire
2027	6 February 2027–25 January 2028	Fire
2028	26 January 2028–12 February 2029	Earth
2029	13 February 2029–2 February 2030	Earth
2030	3 February 2030–22 January 2031	Metal
2031	23 January 2031–10 February 2032	Metal
2032	11 February 2032–30 January 2033	Water
2033	31 January 3033–18 February 2034	Water
2034	19 February 2034–7 February 2035	Wood
2035	8 February 2035–27 January 2036	Wood

Table 1, Continued

Gregorian Calendar year	Chinese Lunar Year	Chi Signature
2036	28 January 2036–14 February 2037	Fire
2037	15 February 2037–3 February 2038	Fire
2038	4 February 2038–23 January 2039	Earth
2039	24 January 2039–11 February 2040	Earth
2040	12 February 2040–31 January 2041	Metal
2041	1 February 2041–21 January 2042	Metal
2042	22 January 2042–9 February 2043	Water
2043	10 February 2043–29 January 2044	Water
2044	30 January 2044–16 February 2045	Wood
2045	17 February 2045–5 February 2046	Wood
2046	6 February 2046–25 January 2047	Fire
2047	26 January 2047–13 February 2048	Fire
2048	14 February 2048–1 February 2049	Earth
2049	2 February 2049–22 January 2050	Earth

Picking a President

This book went to the printer shortly before the U.S. presidential elections on November 7, 2000. Just for the exercise, we tried to predict the winner in advance, using exclusively the theory of chi signature and the five elements. We applied both mundane and transcendental approaches. The chi signature theory was tested in the real world among contemporary negotiators, including some American presidents, and it seemed to work, but we could also apply it to a larger "sample": American presidential candidates.

At first blush, it would seem that presidential rivals do not fit our definition of "negotiators" as we have used it in this book. Instead, they are vying for the support of American voters through town hall meetings, mass rallies, television interviews and the like. Most of the bargaining is actually between the candidate and the potential voter. But they are also debating each other, either indirectly in their campaign speeches or head to head in formal debates—most recently in national televised debates.

From the mundane viewpoint, a candidate during a debate clearly seeks to score points at his opponent's expense. If he is clever—or lucky—the outcome may be scored in his favor. At the transcendental level, however, a candidate may be unwittingly giving an advantage to his opponent, based on the relationship of their respective chi signatures. Let's look at Table 2. Under the "Productive Cycle" category, we could predict a winner by analyzing the auspicious pairings of chi signatures. We know that winners in previous elections had chi signatures that were transcendentally supported by their opponents' chi signatures. For example, in the 1948 elections, Dewey's overconfidence

Table 2. Predicting a Winner

Presidential Candidates	Date of Birth	Chi Signature
"Productive Cycle" Pair		
G.W. Bush	July 6, 1946	Fire
v. Gore	March 31, 1948	Earth
Bush	June 12, 1924	Wood
v. Clinton	August 19, 1946	Fire
Dukakis	November 3, 1933	Water
v. Bush	June 12, 1924	Wood
Ford	July 14, 1913	Water
v. Carter	October 1, 1924	Wood
Humphrey	March 27, 1911	Metal
v. Nixon	January 9, 1913	Water
Dewey	March 24, 1902	Water
v. Truman	May 8, 1884	Wood
Smith	December 30, 1873	Water
v. Hoover	August 10, 1874	Wood
"Destructive Cycle" Pair		
Dole	July 22, 1923	Water
v. Clinton	August 19, 1946	Fire
Mondale	January 5, 1928	Fire
v. Reagan	February 6, 1911	Metal
Carter	October 1, 1924	Wood
v. Reagan	February 6, 1911	Metal
Nixon	January 9, 1913	Water
v. Kennedy	May 29, 1917	Fire
Landon	September 9, 1887	Fire
v. Roosevelt	January 30, 1882	Metal
Hoover	August 10, 1874	Wood
v. Roosevelt	January 30, 1882	Metal
"Non-Cyclical" Pair		
McGovern	July 19, 1922	Water
v. Nixon	January 9, 1913	Water
Goldwater	January 1, 1909	Earth
v. Johnson	August 27, 1908	Earth
Stevenson	February 5, 1900	Metal
v. Eisenhower	October 14, 1890	Metal
Dewey	March 24, 1902	Water
v. Roosevelt	January 30, 1882	Metal
Willkie	February 18, 1892	Water
v. Roosevelt	January 30, 1882	Metal

(and water chi) contributed to the surprise victory of Truman, a wood chi person. The powerful trend shown in Table 2 could only mean that Al Gore would be declared the winner in November, because Vice President Gore possesses an earth chi, which is supported by Governor Bush's fire chi.

The theory cannot predict a winner under the "Destructive Cycle" and "Non-Cyclical" pairings. One reason is that there is no symmetrical cyclic movement; you can't see what's going to happen next with the other pairs. Neither is there a trend regarding the common-sense interaction of the elements; for example, in the 1996 elections Dole's water chi did not extinguish Clinton's fire chi. On the other hand, under the "Productive Cycle," each pair follows the clockwise, cyclic movement of the tai chi symbol (Fig. 16, p. 215)—with the antecedent element facilitating the other member of the pair (as in the accompanying diagram below).

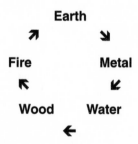

It should be stressed that this theory of chi signatures had a bipartisan set of winners in the past: three Republicans (Bush, Nixon, and Hoover) and three Democrats (Clinton, Carter, and Truman). We will let the reader test this theory on the 2004 elections.

Endnotes

Chapter One: Feng Shui in Action

[1] Colosi, p. 3.

[2] "American soccer mom" is the celebrated stereotypical female from the suburbs who typically balances career and motherhood, and who belongs to a voting bloc sought after by American politicians. Though she may not play soccer herself, she watches her children play the sport; hence, the term "soccer mom."

[3] Mitchell, Janet Lee, "In Out-of-Body Experiences: Is Anything Out?," *Fate*, May 1988, p. 60.

[4] Master Lin Yun has briefly summarized his philosophy in forewords of two books written by his students (Rossbach, 1987, and SantoPietro, 1996).

[5] About a Tibetan religious artifact, a California collector wrote: "Just to hold this sacred object gives the beholder much pleasure. There is an aura of holiness about it that is pervasive. The earth-fossil wax medium that now protects it exudes a fragrance suggestive of incense. With a little imagination and concentration one may hear the striking of bronze gongs and the hoarse chanting of the lamas and monks," Earle J. Stone,

"A Rare Tibetan Folio Cover," *Arts of Asia,* January–February 1980, pp. 138–141.

Chapter Two: Go with the Chi Flow

[1] In aiki-jujutsu, known as jiujitsu in the West, the role of Ki (chi) is central to the execution of *aiki nage*. Davey defines it as "throwing techniques that do not directly use pain or leverage, but rather, throw the opponent through the application of timing, rhythm, centrifugal force, and momentum, as well as by leading his or her Ki (chi)." (p. 149).

[2] Dong and Raffill, pp. 189–190.

Chapter Three: Timing

[1] Following are personal observations of Dr. Anupam N. Shah, an Indian-American computer engineer educated at the University of Michigan, about the negotiating behavior of fellow Gujaratis: "The twenty-four hour period in a day is divided into two twelve-hour periods. Each period is either lucky or unlucky. For each day of the week, these periods are set in a different sequence. Business people would typically consult these periods for negotiations or major transactions, picking the most auspicious time frame."

[2] *Llewellyn's 1999 Moon Sign Book and Gardening Almanac,* p. 37.

Chapter Four: Negotiating for a House Purchase

[1] This prosperous negotiator hosted a dinner for a visiting British entertainer, who then privately published a travelogue illustrated with the layout of the host's residence. Smith, pp. 29–30.

Chapter Five: Bargain Hunting

[1] Abbott, p. 109

Chapter Six: Youth's Unstable Chi

[1] This feng shui approach should be of interest to dream researchers in particular. If you dream about the house you are sleeping in, be careful. It suggests that the chi got out of the body, but, unfortunately, was obstructed by an oppressive structure or interior design feature that prevented it from leaving home to go sightseeing in other places. However, if you spend much time away from home, it is only appropriate that you get homesick and dream of the family house. For example, during the Vietnam War, the enemy had captured a young army captain. This prisoner of war (POW) was then chained to three other POWs to live and work as a chain gang. They maintained and repaired the Ho Chi Minh Trail that was a frequent target of American B-52 bombers. The foursome slept at night in a POW hut, always chained together. The captain frequently dreamed about home and his loved ones. After the war, he returned home, got married, and raised his own family. His dreams did not involve the family home anymore.

Instead, his dreams were mostly sightseeing trips to POW huts near the Ho Chi Minh Trail to check on the welfare of his "close friends." Every time he awoke from such dreams, he would feel a mixture of sadness, panic, and relief.

Chapter Eight: Blessings that Work

[1] Targ and Puthoff, pp. 1–4, 31–34.

[2] Dean, et al, pp. 230–232.

Chapter Ten: How China Lost Hong Kong

[1] At that time "barbarian" (*yuan shi ren*) was the politically correct term in Chinese official usage while "foreign devil" (*yang gui zi*) was deemed a slur. The British resented these names applied to them. They were the world's superpower, and they felt badly treated by the Chinese. Together with other Europeans and Americans, they were allowed to trade with China only at the southern port of Canton in segregated quarters. In addition, they were forbidden to learn the Chinese language, to enter the city center, and to extend their stay beyond the trading season. While "barbarians" were modernizing with the advent of the Industrial Revolution in Europe, America, and Japan, China lagged behind well into the twentieth century.

[2] Swisher, p. 18.

[3] Beeching, p. 136.

[4] Pu-Yi, p. 45.

Chapter Eleven: Diplomacy with Barbarians

[1] Fairbank, p. 57.

[2] Levathes, p. 133.

[3] Levathes, p. 83.

[4] Swisher, p. 45.

[5] Beeching, p. 90.

[6] Swisher, p. 53.

Chapter Twelve: Americans Meet Feng Shui

[1] Fuess, pp. 433–434.

[2] Swisher, p. 174.

Chapter Thirteen: Good-bye to Good Feng Shui

[1] Kissinger, pp. 1058–59.

[2] President Nixon's toast at a banquet in Shanghai with Chairman Chang Ch'un-ch'iao, February 27, 1972: ". . . To mention only one (area of agreement) that is particularly appropriate here in Shanghai, is the fact that this great city, over the past, has on many occasions been the victim of foreign aggression and foreign occupation. And we join the Chinese people, we the American people, in our dedication to this principle: That never again shall foreign domination, foreign occupation, be visited upon this city or any part of China . . ." *Public Papers of the Presidents.*

[3] Han Suyin, p. 381.

⁴ Kissinger, ibid.

⁵ Li, pp. 105–106.

Chapter Fourteen: The Year of the Cat

1 The Vietnamese horoscope is based on the Chinese system of calculation, using the five elements and the twelve animals of the zodiac. Two of these animals were given tropical equivalents: water buffalo in place of ox, and cat instead of rabbit. As in Western astrology, the inputs are place, exact time, day, month, and year of birth. Computer analysis is now the tool of choice.

2 Thieu's astrologer kept a low profile. The author met him for the first time on Oct. 24, 1973, in Saigon. He did not carve out a career as an astrologer, but as a battle-tested army officer under the French, and winner of the *Legion d'Honneur* for bravery and heroism. He was a handsome former mandarin named Colonel Nguyen Van Y (pronounced "eé"), the Director-General of the National Police and concurrently Director of Central Intelligence under President Ngo Dinh Diem. Two days before the coup, Y was on official leave as his wife had just given birth to a baby girl, their eighth child. He was at home during the coup, so that he was immediately purged from the government and sent first to Con Son Island, the penal colony, with "tiger cages" reserved for political prisoners. Later he was moved to Saigon's Chi Hua prison. Y was imprisoned for three and a half years. He

spent his time studying Chinese astrology and developed his expertise by practicing among a captive clientele. He enjoyed the respect of prison authorities, not only for his astrology, but also for his previous role as the country's top policeman. Shortly after his release, he was introduced to Thieu, then planning a presidential bid, by his jailer, General Dang Van Quang, who had been impressed with his astrology. He did not disappoint his client, the presidential hopeful. Later, without naming Y, Thieu told a French journalist in Saigon: " I don't consult astrologers, but horoscopists. Casting horoscopes is a very precise science" (Todd, p. 105). Despite his faith in Y's work, Thieu never asked him to join his government. In fact, Y was never consulted regarding policy decisions that he was about to make. Why Thieu was distrustful and indecisive, astrology alone could not explain. But feng shui could.

[3] Bui Diem, p. 324.

[4] Kissinger, p. 1385.

Chapter Fifteen: Americans Revisit Feng Shui

[1] McCormack, pp. 87–91.

[2] Wilhelm, p. 128.

[3] Hermes, pp. 38–39.

[4] Quoted in Wilhelm, p. 234.

[5] The National Liberation Front, popularly called the Viet Cong, was the North's stalking horse.

They were mostly Southern Communists who returned home after Vietnam's partition to wage guerrilla warfare against the Republic of Vietnam.

[6] Kissinger, pp. 1021–1022.

[7] Karnow, p. 663.

[8] Marshall, pp. 196–197.

[9] Barton Gellman, "Albright gets a Taste of the New Mongolia," *The Washington Post*, May 3, 1998.

Chapter Sixteen: American Power Spot

[1] Manchester, p. 491.

[2] "Reorienting Yourself for Wealth and Power," *The Washington Post*, Oct. 24, 1983.

[2] "Hail to the Chi," *Time Magazine*, Feb. 10, 1997.

[3] Manchester, pp. 490–491.

Chapter Seventeen: Chateau Fleur d'Eau

[1] Fleming, p. 167.

[2] Quigley, p. 139.

[3] Reagan, Nancy, p. 340.

[4] Doris Klein Bacon interview with President Reagan, quoted in Quigley, pp. 145–146.

[5] *Speaking My Mind*, p. 247.

[6] Michael Korda, "Prompting the President," *The New Yorker*, Oct. 6, 1997, pp. 88–95.

[7] Conversation between former U.S. Secretary of State George Shultz and Gorbachev at Stanford University. PBS documentary, *The American Experience: Reagan*, telecast on July 11, 1998.

[8] Reagan, Nancy, p. 342.

[9] Ibid.

[10] *An American Life*, p. 640.

[11] Ibid.

Chapter Eighteen: Fragrant Harbor Waters

[1] Morris, p. 238.

[2] Personal observations by the author on a visit to Hong Kong, April 7–8, 1998.

Chapter Nineteen: Conclusion: Diplomacy Feng Shui-ed

[1] Freeman, pp. 87–92.

[2] Holbrooke, pp. 4, 106, 235, 245, 323.

[3] Solomon, p. 164.

[4] Gerald Segal, "Does China Matter?" *Foreign Affairs*, Sept.–Oct. 1999, p. 24–36.

Glossary

All-under-Heaven: Chinese Empire; also, the Celestial Empire.

Bagua: The logo of feng shui. It is an octagon based on the ancient Chinese book of divination, *The Book of Change.* When this logo is superimposed on a dwelling or office, it is interpreted as a kind of spiritual search warrant. It empowers the feng shui practitioner to uncover hazards to the occupant's wellbeing and to remedy these defects.

Barbarian: A foreigner without any education in Chinese culture and civilization; more likely, European or American, in nineteenth-century Chinese diplomatic usage.

Black Hat Tantric Buddhism: A Chinese cultural borrowing from Tibet, it is one of the four sects of Tibetan Buddhism, distinguishable by the color of the monk's hat. The Black Hat sect has influenced the growing popularity of feng shui in America.

Bodhisattva: In Buddhism, a person who embodies compassion and radiates wisdom gained from direct perception of the truth.

Chai: Food. Sounds the same as the word for money. In Cantonese, *faet choih* means "making money."

Chi: Life force energy. It is an attribute of persons as well their surroundings (man-made structures and the natural environment). Chi can be positive (auspicious) or negative (inauspicious).

Chi adjustment: A way to spiritually transform negative energy to positive energy within a home, in an office or within a person. It is often experienced as high-energy stimulation from exceptional persons or auspicious surroundings.

Chi compatibility: A spiritual dimension, or "heaven luck," in negotiation. Based on a match of antagonists' chi signatures.

Chi gong: A combination of movement exercises and meditation to increase the smooth flow of chi and to concentrate the human spirit.

Ch'i kou: Literally, mouth of the chi. Main door of a house.

Chi signature: Human chi can be characterized as a combination of five elements: fire, earth, metal, water, and wood. But one's date of birth in the Chinese lunar calendar determines which element is optimally expressed, and this element would become the person's chi signature.

Feng shui: The ancient Chinese art of balancing environmental chi with the flow of a person's chi to increase his or her effectiveness in human affairs. Man-made structures are often sources of negative chi. Thus, a new home or workplace needs to be "feng shui-ed."

Ger: Mongol tent made by stretching a piece of thick woolen felt across a squat cylindrical framework of thin wooden struts, deemed a feng shui-correct dwelling because it has one door and no windows (for consensual decision-making in the family), and because of its spiral shape. This shape follows the "natural" tai chi symbol in the center of any home.

Haragei: Japanese for "the art of the belly." A form of nonverbal communication in which a speaker says just a few words but manages to deliver a complex message.

Karma: According to Buddhist and Hindu thought, your fate in the next stage of existence is determined by the balance sheet of good and bad deeds you have done so far, reckoned from your present and past lives. Karmic merit or demerit you earned today will be entered into a ledger for your upward or downward development.

Killing chi: Negative energy emanating from sharp objects or structures. It travels in a straight line, giving bad feng shui to those caught in the line of fire.

Mantra: A prayer or invocation, sometimes held to have magical power. As regenerated sound currents, a mantra raises chi.

Mongols: Nomadic tribes inhabiting an isolated plateau in the heart of Central Asia; In the thirteenth–fourteenth centuries, Mongol armies overran Asia, the Middle East and Eastern Europe; a famous Mongol edifice is India's Taj Mahal; a big filmmaker in Hollywood is called a movie mogul (derived from Mongol).

Mudra: Hand positions to access the flow of positive energy or to get rid of negative energy.

Out of body: Chi becomes a frequent flyer traveling at the speed of thought, away from the vicinity of the physical body, in order to visit distant places, including foreign cities. An example is the paranormal phenomenon of "remote viewing."

Opium War: British military campaign in China, 1840–42, sparked by Beijing's confiscation of illicit opium stocks held by British traders in Canton. After her defeat, China agreed to open to trade five ports, including Canton, and to cede in perpetuity the island of Hong Kong to Britain.

Paranormal: Any phenomenon that defies explanation in terms of acknowledged scientific principles.

"Realist" diplomacy: Pragmatic foreign policy based on realistic accommodation of antagonists; contrasted to "idealist" diplomacy based primarily on appeals to global moral order and to world opinion.

Remote viewing: Experiment whereby a subject is instructed to move his or her viewpoint (but not the body) to a remote location anywhere in the world and to describe what he or she saw. Others, not the experimenter, prepare the map coordinates. The hits are often above chance.

Sat ch'u: In Vietnamese, energy lines "killing the owner of the house;" from the Chinese phrase, Shar Chi for "killing chi."

Shiatsu: A traditional form of Japanese massage for purposes of restoring harmony and balance to the chi of the client. The shiatsu practitioner works at floor level while the client lies fully clothed on a futon. When tension in the hara is released, the flow of chi spreads smoothly toward the arms, the legs, the skin, the head, and the neck.

Tai chi symbol: "Diagram of the Supreme Ultimate" (Fig. 17). In Taoism (pronounced "dow-ism"), the tai chi symbol reflects the cycles of seasons, months, hours, as well as how opposites are not in opposition, but are merely two parts of the one thing. The symmetry suggests a continuous cyclic movement. In a house or office, the tai chi area is the center of balance and health.

Figure 17. Tai chi symbol in Taoism.

Tan den: Chinese for belly, the "seat of the chi;" also hara, in Japanese.

Taoist: A person who seeks the Tao (The Way) via intuitive wisdom rather than through logic and language. Tao core values include harmony with the Way of nature, government keeping a low profile, compassion for the underdog, and a quest for immortality.

Tartar: Nomads who lived alongside the Mongols in eastern Mongolia.

Tet: Vietnamese lunar New Year celebration. Ironically, the first day of Tet starts with the typical family fretting about bad luck entering the house to cause trouble for the rest of the year.

Viet Cong: In the Vietnam War, southern Communists who fought as guerillas, with North Vietnamese support, against the Saigon government.

Zero-sum conflict: Conflict in which the losses of one side are expected to be equal in magnitude to the gains of the other side; opposite of an expected win-win outcome.

Bibliography

Abbott, R. Tucker. *Seashells of the World*. New York: Golden Press, 1962.

Beeching, Jack. *The Chinese Opium Wars*. New York: Harcourt Brace Jovanovich, 1975.

Bui, Diem with David Chanoff. *In the Jaws of History*. Boston: Houghton Mifflin Company, 1987.

Colosi, Thomas R. *On and Off the Record: Colosi on Negotiation*. Washington: American Arbitration Association, 1993.

Davey, H. E. *Unlocking the Secrets of Aiki-jujutsu*. Indianapolis: Masters Press, 1997.

Dean, Douglas, John Mihalasky, Sheila Ostrander, and Lynn Schroeder. *Executive ESP*. Englewood Cliffs, N.J.: Prentice-Hall, 1974.

Dong, Paul and Thomas E. Raffill. *China's Super Psychics*. New York: Marlowe and Company, 1997.

Fairbank, John K. *China Perceived*. New York: Knopf, 1974.

Fleming, Ian. *Thrilling Cities*. New York: Signet Books, 1965.

Freeman, Charles W. *Arts of Power: Statecraft and Diplomacy.* Washington: United States Institute of Peace Press, 1997.

Fuess, Claude M. *The Life of Caleb Cushing.* Vol. I & II. Hampden, Conn.: Archon Books, 1965.

Han Suyin. *Eldest Son: Zhou Enlai and China.* New York: Hill and Wang, 1994.

Hermes, Walter G. *Truce Tent and Fighting Front.* Washington: Office of the Chief of Military History, United States Army, 1966.

Holbrooke, Richard. *To End a War.* New York: Random House, 1998.

Hung, Nguyen Tien and Jerrold Schecter. *The Palace File.* New York: Harper and Row, 1986.

Karnow, Stanley. *Vietnam, A History.* New York: Penguin Books, 1984.

Kissinger, Henry. *White House Years.* Boston: Little, Brown and Company, 1979.

Levathes, Louise. *When China Ruled the Seas.* New York: Oxford Univ. Press, 1994.

Li Zhisui. *The Private Life of Chairman Mao.* New York: Random House, 1994.

Llewellyn's 1999 Moon Sign Book and Gardening Almanac. St. Paul: Llewellyn Publications, 1998.

Manchester, William. *American Caesar.* Boston: Little Brown and Company, 1978.

Marshall, Robert. *Storm from the East.* Berkeley: Univ. of California Press, 1993.

McCormack, Mark H. *On Negotiating*. Beverly Hills: Dove Books, 1995.

Morris, Jan. *Hong Kong*. New York: Random House, 1988.

Pu-Yi. *From Emperor to Citizen*. New York: Oxford Univ. Press, 1987.

Quigley, Joan. *What Does Joan Say? My Seven Years as White House Astrologer to Nancy and Ronald Reagan*. New York: Birch Lane Press, 1990.

Reagan, Nancy, with William Novak. *My Turn*. New York: Random House, 1989.

Reagan, Ronald. *Speaking My Mind*. New York: Simon and Schuster, 1989.

———. *An American Life*. New York: Simon and Schuster, 1990.

Rossbach, Sarah. *Interior Design with Feng Shui*. New York: Arkana, 1991.

Santopietro, Nancy. *Feng Shui by Design*. New York: Perigee Books, 1996.

Smith, Albert. *To China and Back*. Hong Kong: Hong Kong University Press, 1974.

Solomon, Richard H. *Chinese Negotiating Behavior*. Washington: United States Institute for Peace Press, 1999.

Swisher, Earl. *China's Management of the American Barbarians*. New York: Octagon Books, 1972.

Targ, Russell and Harold Puthoff. *Mind Reach: Scientists Look at Psychic Ability*. New York: Delacorte, 1977.

Todd, Olivier. *Cruel April*. New York: Norton, 1990.

Wilhelm, Alfred, Jr. *The Chinese at the Negotiating Table*. Washington: National Defense Univ. Press, 1994.

Index

☽ REACH FOR THE MOON

Llewellyn publishes hundreds of books on your favorite subjects! To get these exciting books, including the ones on the following pages, check your local bookstore or order them directly from Llewellyn.

ORDER BY PHONE

- Call toll-free within the U.S. and Canada, 1-800-THE MOON
- In Minnesota, call (651) 291-1970
- We accept VISA, MasterCard, and American Express

ORDER BY MAIL

- Send the full price of your order (MN residents add 7% sales tax) in U.S. funds, plus postage & handling to:

  Llewellyn Worldwide
  P.O. Box 64383, Dept. 1-56718-038-8
  St. Paul, MN 55164–0383, U.S.A.

POSTAGE & HANDLING

(For the U.S., Canada, and Mexico)
- $4.00 for orders $15.00 and under
- $5.00 for orders over $15.00
- No charge for orders over $100.00

We ship UPS in the continental United States. We ship standard mail to P.O. boxes. Orders shipped to Alaska, Hawaii, The Virgin Islands, and Puerto Rico are sent first-class mail. Orders shipped to Canada and Mexico are sent surface mail.

International orders: Airmail—add freight equal to price of each book to the total price of order, plus $5.00 for each non-book item (audio tapes, etc.).

Surface mail—Add $1.00 per item.

Allow 2 weeks for delivery on all orders.
Postage and handling rates subject to change.

DISCOUNTS

We offer a 20% discount to group leaders or agents. You must order a minimum of 5 copies of the same book to get our special quantity price.

FREE CATALOG

Get a free copy of our color catalog, *New Worlds of Mind and Spirit*. Subscribe for just $10.00 in the United States and Canada ($30.00 overseas, airmail). Many bookstores carry *New Worlds*—ask for it!

Visit our website at www.llewellyn.com for more information.

101 FENG SHUI TIPS FOR THE HOME

Richard Webster

For thousand of years, people in the Far East have used feng shui to improve their home and family lives and live in harmony with the earth. People who practice feng-shui achieve a deep contentment that is denied most others. They usually do well romantically and financially. Even people like Donald Trump freely admit to using feng shui.

Now you can make subtle and inexpensive changes to your home that can literally transform your life. If you're in the market for a house, learn what to look for in room design, single level vs. split level, staircases, front door location, and more. If you want to improve upon your existing home, find out how its current design may be creating negative energy, and discover simple ways to remedy the situation without the cost of major renovations or remodeling.

Watch your success and spirits soar when you discover:
- How to evaluate the current feng shui energy in your home
- Why you must make a concentrated effort to discard anything that you are storing and not using
- How the shape and slope of your driveway may be sending good luck *away* from your house
- What to do about negative energy from neighbors
- How to use fountains or aquariums to attract money
- The best position for the front door
- The best color to paint your kitchen
- Colors to use and avoid for each member of the family

1-56718-809-5, 192 pp., 5¼ x 8, charts   **$9.95**

FENG SHUI FOR SUCCESS & HAPPINESS

Richard Webster

"If you want to be happy," a wise man once said, "be happy!" However, it is not always easy to remain happy when your environment is working against you. Your home should be a place where you can completely be yourself. You should be able to relax there and forget all the cares and problems of the outside world. Consequently, many of your happiest moments should be spent in your home.

The ancient Chinese noticed that different environments had a direct bearing on contentment and even luck. Later on, these factors would become known as feng shui, the art of living in harmony with the earth. Whether you live in a one-room apartment or a sprawling mansion, *Feng Shui for Success & Happiness* (part of Richard Webster's Feng Shui series), will show you how to activate the energy, or ch'i, in your home to improve your environment and to achieve happiness and abundance.

1-56718-815-X, 168 pp., 5¼ x 8, illus.   **$9.95**

Spanish edition:
FENG SHUI PARA EL ÉXITO Y LA FELICIDAD

1-56718-820-6   **$7.95**

CHINESE HEALTH CARE SECRETS
A Natural Lifestyle Approach

Henry B. Lin

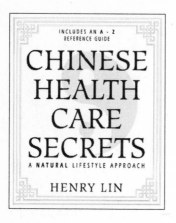

At a time when the medical costs in this country are sky-rocketing and chronic disease runs rampant in every walk of life, *Chinese Health Care Secrets* offers a readily applicable, completely natural, and highly effective alternative. It serves as a practical reference on personal health care, as well as a textbook on a health care system from the world's oldest civilization. The Chinese belief is that you can achieve optimal health by carrying out your daily activities—including diet, sleep, emotional feeling, physical exercise, and sexual activity—according to the laws of Nature. It is especially effective in treating the degenerative diseases that plague millions of Americans.

Many of the techniques have never before been published, and are considered secrets even in China. Avoid common ailments brought on by aging and modern society when you take charge of your own health with age-old Chinese wisdom, including:

- The secrets of proper diet, sleep and rest, physical hygiene, mental discipline, regular exercise, regulated sex, environmental hygiene
- A list of sixty-five of nature's potent healers
- Secrets of sexual vitality, rejuvenation, and longevity
- The road to immortality
- An A-Z reference guide of special solutions for seventy-six of the most common health problems

1-56718-434-0, 528 pp., 7½ x 9⅛, illus.   **$24.95**

TO ORDER, CALL 1-800-THE MOON
Prices subject to change without notice.

THE ART & SCIENCE OF FENG SHUI

The Ancient Chinese Tradition of Shaping Fate

Henry B. Lin

The art of feng shui has exerted a profound influence on China's landform and the Chinese mind for 3,000 years. Now wildly popular in the West, feng shui has reached the point where readers want more in-depth information based on classical theory.

True feng shui is more malleable and fluid than the feng shui popularized by most Western authors. It is not a strict science with standard rules; it is an art that demands intuition, imagination, and creative understanding.

Henry Lin, a native of China, offers deep insight into how feng shui fits within the framework of history and Taoist thought. He shows how a variety of circumstances (from the lay of the land to the homeowner's birth year) can affect other important issues (i.e., how a particular house impacts a particular resident).

Full of practical advice, the book teaches how to notice geographic qi when surveying a landsite, how to find the right residential or commercial property for you, and ways to countermeasure irregularities and deficiencies.

1-56718-436-7, 336 pp., 7½ x 9⅛, 53 illus. $17.95

A complete self-teaching guide

P. SCOTT
HOLLANDER

HANDWRITING ANALYSIS
A Complete Self-Teaching Guide

P. Scott Hollander
(Formerly titled
Reading Between the Lines)

Anyone who reads and follows the procedures in *Handwriting Analysis* will come away with the ability to take any sample of handwriting and do a complete analysis of character and personality. He or she may even go forward to use the skill as a professional tool, or as the basis for a profession.

This self-teaching textbook demonstrates how to analyze handwriting, how to counsel others, and how best to use the subject once learned. Unlike the many "cookbook" graphology books on the market, this book gives a very thorough and considered approach to the subject.

Handwriting Analysis can help you gain insight into your own strengths and weaknesses and can provide a means to make wiser decisions in your personal and professional life. You will have a quick, sure means of discovering what someone else is really like, and you can use graphotherapy to effect character and personality changes.

Handwriting Analysis also contains an excellent section on the writing of children, and an Index of Traits which summarizes and reiterates points made in the book for quick reference.

1-56718-390-5, 336 pp., 7 x 10   **$14.95**

PALMISTRY
The Whole View

Judith Hipskind

Here is a unique approach to palmistry! Judy Hipskind not only explains how to analyze hands, but also explains why hand analysis works. The approach is based on a practical rationale and is easy to understand. Over 130 illustrations accompany the informal, positive view of hand analysis.

This new approach to palmistry avoids categorical predictions and presents the meaning of the palm as a synthesis of many factors: the shape, gestures, flexibility, mounts, and lives of each hand—as well as a combination of the effects of both heredity and the environment. No part of the hand is treated as a separate unit; the hand reflects the entire personality. An analysis based on the method presented in this book is a rewarding experience for the client—a truly whole view!

0-87542-306-X, 248 pp., 5¼ x 8, illus.   **$9.95**

THE NEW WAY TO LEARN ASTROLOGY
Presenting the Noel Tyl Method
Basil Fearrington

The most celebrated astrologer of our time, Noel Tyl, has educated a generation of astrologers with his holistic and psychological approach. Now, his power-packed method is offered in this home-study course for beginners, exactly as it's taught at the Noel Tyl Study Center for Astrology and New Age Exploration in South Africa.

Students of Tyl's classroom course learn the basics of sophisticated analytical techniques in just eighty hours. With *The New Way to Learn Astrology*, you can take the same course—at your own pace—and assess your progress with the test questions provided at the end of each chapter. (Compare your answers with those of Noel Tyl himself!)

You need no previous knowledge of astrology to begin this course. You will progress from the planets and signs to aspects, parental tensions, the Sun-Moon Blend, and secondary progressions. Go beyond doing mere "readings" to conducting professional "consultations," an enriching discussion with clients about their lives, using astrological symbolism as your guide.

1-56718-739-0, 264 pp., 7½ x 9⅛　　　　　　**$14.95**

NUMEROLOGY FOR BEGINNERS
Easy Guide to Love • Money • Destiny

Gerie Bauer

Every letter and number in civilization has a particular power, or vibration. For centuries, people have read these vibrations through the practice of numerology. References in the Bible even describe Jesus using numerology to change the names of his disciples. *Numerology for Beginners* is a quick ready-to-use reference that lets you find your personal vibrations based on the numbers associated with your birthdate and name.

Within minutes, you will be able to assess the vibrations surrounding a specific year, month, and day—even a specific person. Detect whether you're in a business cycle or a social cycle, and whether a certain someone or occupation would be compatible with you. Plus, learn to detect someone's personality within seconds of learning their first name!

1-56718-057-4, 336 pp., 5³⁄₁₆ x 8   **$9.95**

THE OFFICE ORACLE
Wisdom at Work
Patricia Monaghan

A strategy manual in the tradition of Machiavelli, Sun Tzu's *The Art of War*, and Tom Peters' *In Pursuit of Excellence*, *The Office Oracle* provides fast, savvy advice to help you skillfully master all of work's challenges.

With three quick tosses of four coins, you can become a workplace wizard. *The Office Oracle* will lead you to the appropriate lesson you need to ponder. Learn when you should smile and when to attack, when to take advantage of career opportunities, how to make money in the gray areas, and 197 other shrewd strategies for success.

Refuse to sleep through the marvelous flow and flux that surrounds you. Open your eyes to the multiple possibilities of every occasion. Learn to detect change as it is about to occur and use it to your advantage. Become one of the wise with the help of *The Office Oracle*.

1-56718-464-2, 224 pp., 5¼ x 6   **$7.95**

PREDICTING EVENTS WITH ASTROLOGY

Celeste Teal

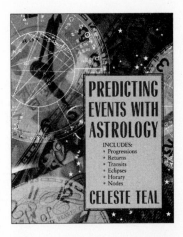

Now anyone who understand the basics of astrology can learn how to see into the progressed chart of any individual and determine the trends and events likely to transpire at any given time. More than any other book on the market, *Predicting Events with Astrology* simplifies the techniques by demonstrating their use through factual case histories and chart delineation. In each event, the story unfolds with the technical concepts in a way that is as easy to grasp as it is entertaining.

You will come to know certain signature aspects, such as Jupiter with Neptune for wealth and squares between Pluto and Mars for accidents. You'll master the meaning of a natal conjunction of Pluto and the North Node, and what it means to have Venus as the first natal planet to rise to the transiting ascendant.

1-56718-704-8, 288 pp., 7½ x 9⅛ **$14.95**

TAROT FOR BEGINNERS
An Easy Guide to Understanding & Interpreting the Tarot

P. Scott Hollander

The Tarot is much more than a simple divining tool. While it can—and does—give you accurate and detailed answers to your questions when used for fortunetelling, it can also lead you down the road to self-discovery in a way that few other meditation tools can do. *Tarot for Beginners* will tell you how to use the cards for meditation and self-enlightenment as well as for divination.

If you're just beginning a study of the Tarot, this book gives you a basic, straightforward definition of the meaning of each card that can be easily applied to any system of interpretation, with any Tarot deck, using any card layout. The main difference between this book and other books on the Tarot is that it's written in plain English—you need no prior knowledge of the Tarot or other arcane subjects to understand its mysteries, because this no-nonsense guide will make the symbolism of the Tarot completely accessible to you. You will receive an overview of of the cards of the Major and Minor Arcana in terms of their origin, purpose, and interpretive uses as well as clear, in-depth descriptions and interpretations of each card.

1-56718-363-8, 352 pp., 5¼ x 8, illus.   **$12.95**

Spanish edition:
TAROT PARA PRINCIPIANTES
1-56718-399-9, 288 pp., 6 x 9, illus.   **$12.95**

WHAT YOUR FACE REVEALS
Chinese Secrets of Face Reading

Henry B. Lin

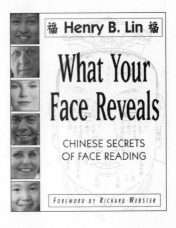

Your forehead may be very promising, but if its color is dark or pale, then summer will be a time of trouble. Your friend with the horse-shaped face is clever, loyal, and will eventually hold a position of great power. Take a good look at your nose—it will tell you whether or not you will be happy in marriage!

The Chinese have been reading faces for more than 3,000 years. Now you can learn how to decode the secrets of fate as written on your face with this simple pictorial guide. Determine the personality of strangers, uncover your future and the future of your loved ones, and use this knowledge to benefit you in work, health, and love.

You will learn how to analyze the shape of the face, its color and spirit, and specific features such as ears, eyebrows, eyes, nose, cheekbones, mouth, teeth, chin, hair, moles, lines, and more. You will also learn a shortcut to face reading with the system of the Twelve Palaces for those times when you only need a broad summary of someone's fate.

1-56718-433-2, 264 pp., 7½ x 9⅛, 150 illus.   **$17.95**

YOUR HEALTH
It's a Question of Balance
Dr. Igor Cetojevic with
Francesca Pinoni

If you're one of the growing number of people beginning to look into alternative therapies, then this quick-reading introduction to Chinese medicine, electromagnetic vibrations, and the use of gemstones in healing is just what the doctor ordered—Dr. Cetojevic, that is, who explains it all in terms even a child can understand.

Trained in both Western and Eastern medicine, Dr. Cetojevic shows you how to improve your health by following the principles of Yin (cold, dark) and Yang (hot, light) to tailor your diet and lifestyle to your individual constitution. See how your body's organs correlate with the time of day and seasons of the year, and how you can use that knowledge to improve your own health and well-being. (For example, if you always wake up at 3 a.m., you may have a weakness in your liver and can benefit from eating more fresh greens and protein.)

Your Health is full of practical advice you can use immediately, including how to use a quartz crystal to make wine taste better and eliminate hangovers, and how to improve your sleep just by moving your bed!

1-56718-121-X, 192 pp., 5³⁄₁₆ x 8, 41 illus.   **$12.95**